100 INVENTIONS
THAT SHAPED WORLD HISTORY

BILL YENNE
DR. MORTON GROSSER, Consulting Editor

sourcebooks
eXplore

Copyright © 1993, 2023 by Sourcebooks
Text by Bill Yenne
Cover design by Will Riley
Internal illustrations by Westchester Publishing Services
Cover and internal design © 2023 by Sourcebooks

Published by Sourcebooks eXplore, an imprint of Sourcebooks Kids
P.O. Box 4410, Naperville, Illinois 60567-4410
(630) 961-3900
sourcebookskids.com

Originally published in 1993 by Bluewood Books, a division of The Siyeh Group, Inc.

Cataloging-in-Publication Data is on file with the Library of Congress.

Source of Production: Versa Press, East Peoria, Illinois, USA
Date of Production: August 2023
Run Number: 5033352

Printed and bound in the United States of America.
VP 10 9 8 7 6 5 4 3 2 1

CONTENTS

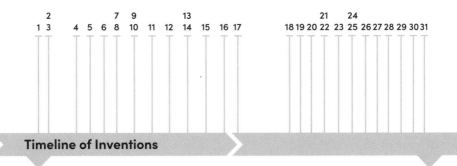

Timeline of Inventions

3.3 million BCE   1750

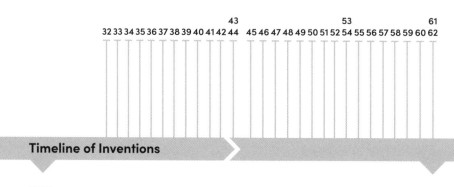

43

53

61

32 33 34 35 36 37 38 39 40 41 42 44   45 46 47 48 49 50 51 52 54 55 56 57 58 59 60 62

Timeline of Inventions

1750

1895

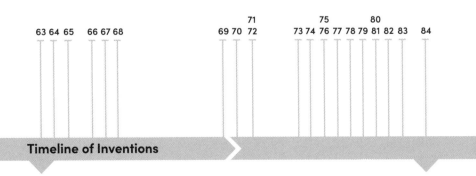

63 64 65   66 67 68   69 70   71 72   73 74   75 76 77 78 79   80 81 82 83   84

Timeline of Inventions

1895   1955

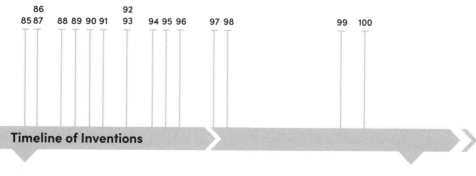

86
85 87   88 89 90 91   92
                                93   94 95 96   97 98   99   100

Timeline of Inventions

1955   **2020**

INTRODUCTION

We humans have distinguished ourselves with our ability to think, to reason, and to fashion tools and build machines that help us in our work—in other words, we *invent*. We use tools to extend or expand our capabilities. Over the centuries, such tools have been devised by both individuals and groups, and most have led to other inventions based on the principles of their predecessors.

This book is a capsule of some of the most important milestones in the history of technology, and the selections were based on the following criteria: 1) What kind of impact did the invention have on civilization after it was put into widespread use? 2) Did it change the way we see ourselves as a species? 3) Did it open the door to other inventions? 4) Did it affect our daily lives in a ubiquitous way?

The goal is to present these milestones in their historical context and to give you some basic information about how they came to be, who made them possible, and why they were important. Some inventions have evolved into more advanced versions while others remain more or less in their original form today. Some of the experiments that led to certain inventions can be duplicated at home, but in other cases, the inventions still seem amazingly complex. Many of the most basic inventions were created simultaneously throughout the world. Production and use of fire was achieved in many places on Earth before the earliest recorded history. The same is true of tools such as knives used for hunting. Other inventions that we take for granted existed for centuries in one place, but strangely, were never discovered elsewhere. One good example is the wheel, which had been used in numerous applications from turning pots to moving vehicles for nearly five thousand years in the Eastern Hemisphere. However, when the first European explorers crossed the Atlantic, they discovered that no one in the Americas—not even the highly evolved Aztec and Inca cultures—had yet invented the wheel!

The wheel (turning on its axle) is one of what are known as the six simple machines. These are the basic components upon which countless other machines and engineering projects of greater complexity are based. Three involve linear motion, and three involve circular motion. The first three are the inclined plane, the wedge (which is an extension of the inclined plane concept), and the lever. The rotating machines are the wheel, the pulley (which evolved from the wheel), and the screw. Each of these inventions increased the power and capability of its inventor and their successors, and each is partially or wholly present in the machines we use daily. Imagine how different the world would be today without the six simple machines.

A glance into the future suggests that many exciting technologies will add new milestones to this list. Over a century ago, someone said that everything that could be invented had already been invented. But nothing could have been further from the truth. While forecasting the future is difficult, one thing we can count on is that the centuries to come will be filled with countless wondrous inventions.

Today, saying something is from the stone age suggests that it is incredibly crude or outdated. However, the beginning of the **Stone Age**, the **Paleolithic Period**, was the time when humans first distinguished themselves from virtually all other animals. When our earliest ancestors first learned how to use and make stone implements to help make their work easier, humankind started down the road toward civilization.

Exactly where and when humans first made **stone tools** will probably never be known as archaeologists continue to discover tools that are older than those previously recorded. The oldest known purposefully edged tool—literally the oldest knife blade—was discovered in Africa in 1969 and is estimated to be 2.6 million years old.

It seems likely that people in widely separated places in Asia, Africa, and Europe discovered how to make tools independently of one another, and this may have happened in numerous places 2.4 million years ago.

The earliest stone tools were probably used for hunting and food processing. They included knives, spear points, scrapers, and simple composite grinders for grain—a round rock used in a shallow hole inside of another larger rock. Such a tool was the precursor of the mortar and pestle, which was commonly used to grind grain at home

up until the nineteenth century. It is still used in the pharmaceutical industry today.

Stone knives and scrapers were the forerunners of the metal implements that are so familiar to us today. Their shapes are recognizably related, and a sharp flint or obsidian knife is still a useful tool and a dangerous weapon.

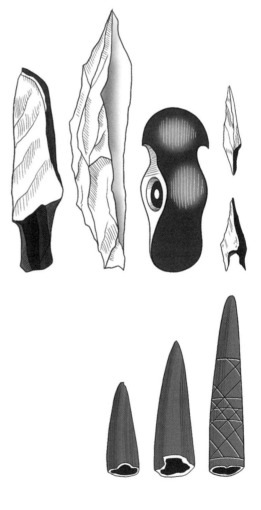

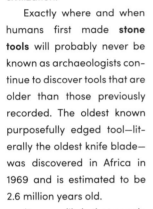

RESISTANCE

FORCE

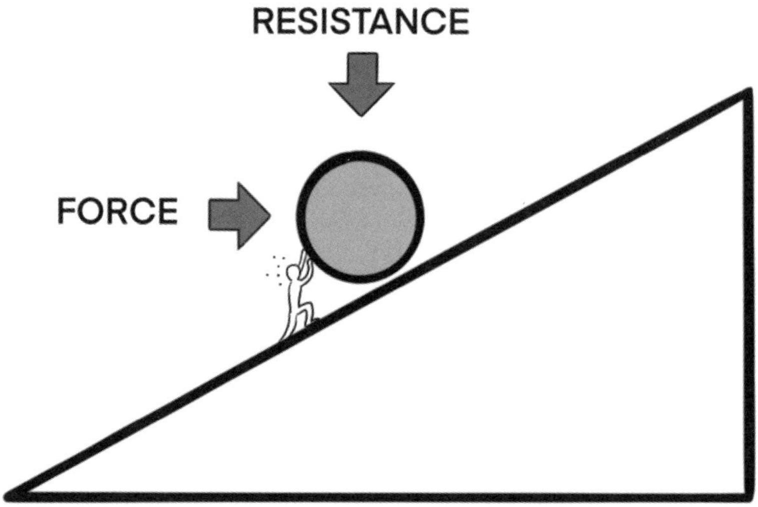

The **inclined plane**, believed to have been in use longer than any of the other basic machines, is based on a simple concept: When an object must be moved from a lower elevation to a higher one, more power is required to move it up a steeper slope than a shallow one. This is true whether we are moving our own bodies when climbing, pushing a solid object, propelling a wheeled vehicle, or driving a motorized one. The shallower the slope, the less power is required.

Ancient humans discovered that it was easier to drag objects up a slope than to pull them straight up a cliff. Eventually, they realized that if a slope did not exist, they could build one by leaning logs or poles against a steep incline to make it shallower. They also discovered that they could pile dirt or rocks against a cliff and create a permanent inclined plane. Egyptian builders used such inclined planes in major construction projects, such as the pyramids.

Planes built at specific inclinations, or **grades**, have been utilized in road building for centuries, and they are still used today. Staircases are also a form of inclined planes, as are accessibility ramps for people who use wheelchairs to bypass staircases.

Force

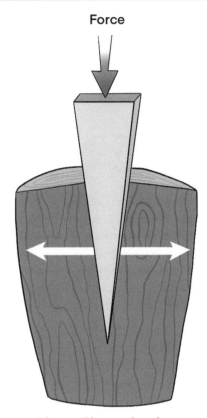

**A downward force produces forces
perpendicular to its inclined surfaces**

One of the **six basic machines**, the wedge is a version of the inclined plane. The wedge can be described as a double inclined plane whose narrow end is inserted into another substance in order to split it into two parts.

Stone knives were possibly the first wedge-type tools. Wedges for splitting wood are the simplest ones, and axes and chisels are variations on this principle. Shovels are wedges, and nails are also based on the wedge principle. A shovel breaks up a solid mass of gravel or dirt, just as a traffic divider splits the fluid mass of individual vehicles. Thus, a traffic divider can also be considered a type of a wedge.

It has been said that civilization began when human beings were first able to produce and control fire for their own benefit. Before that time, **fire** must have been seen as a terrible and frightening destroyer.

Somehow, in the distant mists of time, prehistoric humans in widely scattered parts of the world learned that fire had the power to warm as well as harm. Eventually, humans determined that small, controlled fires could make their environment more comfortable when it was cold and enable them to see in the dark. This made it a gathering place.

The next step might have been discovering that cooked food often tasted better and lasted longer than uncooked food. Fire also came to be used as both an offensive and a defensive weapon, and ultimately as a tool in metalworking and ceramics.

For many centuries, the origin of fire remained a mystery. Fires could be moved and transported. They could be made smaller and made larger, but when they died, they could not be revived. The only way to start a fire was with another fire, or by waiting for lightning to strike. As civilization evolved, fire took on a mystical significance, and a designated "keeper of the fire" in each society had an important role because they maintained the master fire with which other smaller fires could be ignited and fed.

Eventually—possibly around 500,000 BCE—a means of starting fires was found. This happened independently throughout the world in modern-day Europe, Africa, Asia, Australia, and the Americas. By the Age of Discovery in the sixteenth century, fire making was understood almost everywhere on Earth, although some records tell of encounters with isolated, primitive peoples who had not yet mastered the art of making fire as recent as the nineteenth century.

The earliest methods of starting fires included various techniques of friction, such as rubbing two pieces of wood together. In North America, the Iroquois and Inuit peoples built sturdy and efficient drill-like devices with which fires could be easily started. The next step in the evolution of fire was the use of flint struck upon steel. Other early human societies in Southeast Asia invented the more sophisticated "fire piston," consisting of a bamboo tube and a plunger.

As it grew more controllable, fire became a central feature of human life because of its importance in heating and cooking, its social significance, and its role in the development of many subsequent inventions that would come to define modern civilizations.

The **bow and arrow** weapon system has been used by humans since prehistoric times. Invented before 50,000 BCE, it is still used by a number of remote human societies as a primary weapon and by many cultures as a sporting arm.

The primitive bow was a long, slender rod of wood or bamboo bent into an arc by a cord—the **bowstring**—stretched between its ends. The **arrow** is a slim, straight shaft of wood, bamboo, or similar material fitted with a slotted tip—the **nock**—to engage the bowstring at the rear. It has a sharp point of fire-hardened wood, stone, shell, or metal at the front of the **arrowhead**. Feathers, vanes, or other **flights** may be fitted at the rear to help the arrow fly straight.

In use, an arrow is placed across the bow with the string in the nock, and the bowstring is drawn back until the arrow spans the full length from the string to the bow. When the string is released, the energy stored in the bent fibers of the bow is transmitted through the taut bowstring to the rear of the arrow, accelerating it forward at a high speed.

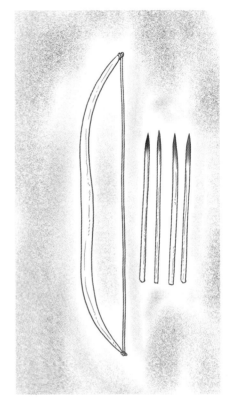

The simple bow has been made in many styles and from many materials. Its most famous form is probably the six-foot **English longbow** of the fourteenth and fifteenth centuries, which was usually made of yew or Osage orange wood and proved to be a highly effective weapon in England's battles with the French at Crécy in 1346 and Agincourt in 1415. Meanwhile, in Asia and the Middle East, the **compound bow** was developed. This shorter, reverse-curve bow used horn, gut, or other stiff elastic materials that were laminated to the front of the bow. This increased its resistance to bending, and hence, increased its available power. The shorter length made compound bows easier to shoot from horseback, and they became the main weapons of many horse-mounted peoples.

The idea of stiffening the bow was carried further in the **crossbow**, which uses a short, very powerful bow mounted on a stock similar to a rifle. The crossbow was first developed in China, in both rifle and pistol form, by the Han dynasty (206 BCE–220 CE). Although early crossbows could be cocked by hand, later versions needed external ratchets or levers to pull back their thick bowstrings. The crossbow was released by a trigger and could propel its short and heavy arrow—or **bolt**—with great force, making it able to pierce some medieval armor.

Most forms of the bow are still being made, and modern bows can send an arrow forward a tremendous distance. The compound bow has a range of over 1,000 feet; the recurve bow has a range of over 800 feet; and the crossbow can shoot up to 1,500 feet!

Wind **instruments** probably originated before the dawn of history. Examples of pre-historic, primitive **flutes** have been found in the form of animal bones with holes drilled in them. Egyptian and Sumerian flutes from around 3000 BCE have also been unearthed, and such wind instruments have continued to evolve to the present day. The French composer **Jean Baptiste Lully** wrote the earliest known flute music in 1681, and Theobald Boehm in Germany perfected the modern-day flute in the nineteenth century by designing the hole and key placement that is still used today.

The **horn**, in its basic form, is also a prehistoric invention. Originally, horns were literally animal horns, and seashells and animal tusks were used for horns in various parts of the world. The **trumpet** evolved from the horn and is also quite old. A bronze trumpet from 2000 BCE was found in Egypt, and the practice of rolling the tube into a loop, as is common with modern brass instruments, was known to both the Romans and the early Scandinavians. Valves were first added to horns in the early nineteenth century.

The **oboe**, which uses a res-onating double reed, is based on Egyptian instruments from 2000 BCE. However, its present form was created by Frédéric Triébert in France in the nine-teenth century. The **clarinet**, a single reed instrument, was invented by Johann Christoph Denner in Nuremberg, Germany, around 1670. Variations of this instrument also existed in

ancient Egypt and Greece. The **bassoon**, which was first identified in the seventeenth century, is probably of Celtic origin.

The **saxophone**, one of the most recent wind instruments, was developed in Belgium by Antoine-Joseph "Adolphe" Sax while he was working on a means of improving the bass clarinet. Patented in 1846, it was a popular instrument seen in military bands, and composers such as Hector Berlioz and Gioacchino Rossini used it before the saxo-phone became a key element in **jazz** music starting in the 1920s.

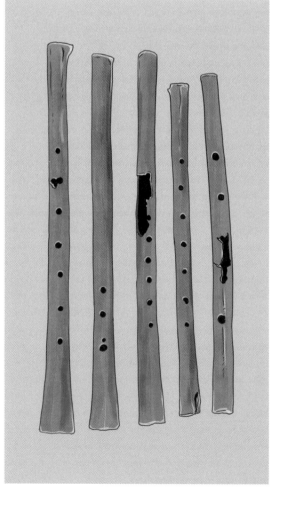

Nearly every machine built since the beginning of the **Industrial Revolution** involves a single, basic principle embodied in one of humankind's truly significant inventions. Indeed, it's hard to imagine any mechanized system that would be possible without the **wheel** or some kind of symmetrical component moving in a circular motion on an axis. From tiny watch gears to automobiles, jet engines, and computer disk drives, the principle is the same.

Based on diagrams inscribed into ancient clay tablets, the earliest known use of this essential invention was the potter's wheel used in the Mesopotamian city of Ur as early as 3500 BCE, and the first use of the wheel for transportation was probably on Mesopotamian chariots in 3200 BCE. It is interesting to note that wheels may have had industrial or manufacturing applications before they were used on vehicles.

The spoked wheel first appeared on Egyptian chariots around 2000 BCE, and wheels seem to have developed in Europe by 1400 BCE without any outside influence. Because the idea of the wheel appears so simple, it's easy to assume that the wheel would have simply come to be in every culture when it reached a particular level of development. However, this is not the case. As noted earlier, the great Inca, Aztec, and Maya civilizations reached an extremely high level of sophistication, yet they never used the wheel. In fact, there is no evidence that the use of the wheel existed among early peoples anywhere in the Western Hemisphere until well after contact with Europeans.

Even in Europe, the wheel evolved little until the beginning of the nineteenth century. However, with the coming of the Industrial Revolution, the wheel became a core technology and was used in thousands of ways and in countless different mechanisms.

The simplest form of **sundial**, the oldest known means of telling time, was a vertical stick placed upright in the ground so that it cast a shadow. Later sundials often took the form of a flat panel with the hours of the day marked on it and used a vertical blade, called a **gnomon**, to cast the shadow. The use of the moving shadow was a means of tracking the progress of the day. This technology was invented independently by both the Chinese and the Chaldeans about 3500 BCE.

One version of the sundial with a small, circular plate beneath the gnomon has been attributed to Greek philosopher and astronomer Anaximander of Miletus, who is thought to have made the first one sometime during his life, between 610 and 546 BCE.

Stone tools and the wheel gave humankind the ability to master physical obstacles in the environment. Also innate in humans was the abstract reasoning power to work with that environment on a conceptual level. Humans are capable of counting, adding, subtracting, and solving simple and complex mathematical problems. This ability, which is always present, took time to develop. Eventually, our ancestors mastered mathematics and put it to work in numerous applications, from commerce to engineering.

The **abacus**, one of humankind's oldest machines, is an analog bead-and-wire counting and calculating computer, whose earliest form is thought by some to have come into being around 3000 BCE in Mesopotamia as a sand-covered board in which marks were made with a finger or a stick. In fact, the name abacus derives from an ancient Hebrew word for **"dust."** The system evolved as a grooved board and ultimately reached its wire-and-bead form in Egypt by about 500 BCE. The abacus was also found in Greece and India, and it was in widespread use in China by 190 CE, where it is still commonly used alongside modern calculators.

The Chinese style of abacus, or *suànpán*, uses ten wires with seven beads each to represent place values. One set of beads represents ones and others represent fives. By quickly moving the beads, a skilled abacus user can do addition, subtraction, multiplication, and division as fast as the average person can work similar problems on an electronic calculator.

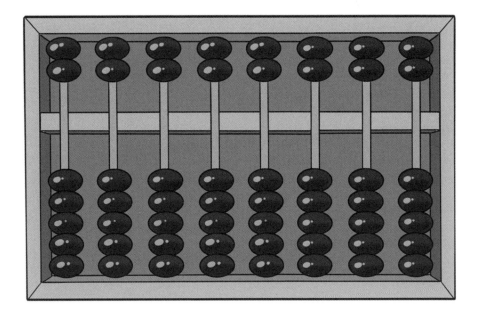

The **harp** or **lyre** is probably the oldest stringed instrument, dating back to the third millennium BCE. Basically a set of strings of various lengths stretched on a frame, these instruments are mentioned in the Bible and Greek mythology and appear in ancient Egyptian and Chinese paintings. There are Egyptian harps in the British Museum in London that have been dated to 1500 BCE. The **double-action pedal harp**, used in today's symphony orchestras, was invented by Sébastien Érard, a French maker of musical instruments. It was embraced immediately by such composers as Hector Berlioz, Franz Liszt, and Richard Wagner.

The **lute** and similar handheld, plucked stringed instruments originated in the Middle Ages. The bowed lute evolved into the viol family and eventually into the **violin**, which originated in France in 1529. The violin maker's art reached its peak in the first decade of the eighteenth century with the work of Antonio Stradivari, a.k.a. the Stradivarius brand, whose craftsmanship has never been equaled.

The first iteration of the modern **bow**, which is used to play violins and other related stringed instruments such as the **viola** and **cello**, was developed by Arcangelo Corelli and Giuseppe Tartini.

The **guitar** developed from the medieval **gittern** and the Renaissance **vihuela**. It was probably introduced to Spain by the Arabs and was established throughout Europe by the late fourteenth century. It rose in popularity during the seventeenth century as an instrument that was easier to play than the fashionable lute, and it has remained a favorite ever since.

The modern form of the guitar was invented around 1850 by the Spanish instrument maker Antonio de Torres, and the basic **acoustic guitar** has remained roughly the same since then. The **electric guitar** was invented in 1931 by Adolph Rickenbacker and George Beauchamp, heads of the Electro String Instrument Corporation in California, but the widespread use of the electric guitar began with the advent of rock 'n' roll in the mid-1950s.

According to a popular legend, which originated with the Roman writer Pliny the Elder, the Phoenicians—or Egyptian sailors on a beach in Phoenicia—invented **glass** by accident. It happened when blocks of **natron** (**hydrated sodium carbonate**) were used to support a cooking pot over a fire built on the **sand**. The heat from the fire was hot enough to melt the two ingredients, and they flowed together to form glass.

The oldest piece of glass known to exist dates back to the time of the Egyptian Pharaoh Amenhotep I, who reigned from 1514–1493 BCE. It is believed to have been made in Egypt or Mesopotamia using the same ingredients mentioned in Pliny's legend. Regardless of whether or not they had invented glass, by about 1200 BCE, the Phoenicians became well-known throughout the Mediterranean region for high-quality glassware that they manufactured for export. Early glassware was formed in molds, but around 250 BCE, the Syrians introduced glassblowing. By the next century, the Romans had embraced the art of **glassblowing** on a large scale, making glassware less expensive and more widely available.

High-quality, very **transparent glass** called *cristallo* was invented in 1463 by a Venetian glassblower from the island of Murano. Crystal, the form of glass which emulates natural quartz by adding lead oxide, was invented in 1675 in England as an alternative to *cristallo*. **Automated glassblowing** for bottles was invented by Michael J. Owens of Toledo, Ohio, and his process was patented on February 26, 1895. The method of producing large, flat plates of glass for **windows** was discovered in 1910 simultaneously by Irving W. Colburn in the United States and Émile Fourcault in Belgium.

A glassworks building from the late eighteenth century

Some profoundly important breakthrough inventions are not things but ways of analyzing our relationship with our environment and ourselves. One such important concept was embodied in the text of the **Hippocratic oath**.

The Greek physician Hippocrates saw disease as a natural process that developed in logical steps, like the acts of a Greek play. Moreover, he saw the patient as an individual whose constitution would react to disease in its own way. This revolutionary concept was neglected for centuries, but it has taken on increasing importance in modern times.

Hippocrates viewed the physician as a man of science instead of a priest. The Hippocratic doctor observed disease, classified it, and predicted its course. He practiced medicine in accordance with the laws of science—as far as science existed at the time—and felt that he himself was bound by the ethical precepts of his profession.

Hippocrates recognized that broken parts must be aligned for normal mending. Traction had to be applied to both ends of a fracture, and then released gradually as the parts fitted together. As always, he urged the doctor to look beyond the local fracture to the patient's total reaction. Mobilization was recommended at an early stage, since "exercise strengthens and inactivity wastes." Today, this maxim is still followed to avoid disuse atrophy.

Greek physician Hippocrates

Like the wheel, the **lever** is one of the six simple machines found in many other more complex mechanisms. The principle of the lever was probably known in prehistoric times, but it was first fully described by the great Greek mathematician Archimedes around 260 BCE.

By definition, a lever is a rigid rod used for lifting. It pivots on a fixed point called a fulcrum. The force applied at one point can be balanced by an appropriate force applied at another point, usually opposite the **fulcrum**. The basic idea of the lever can be illustrated through the example of a crowbar used to raise a heavy object. For a given length of lever, the closer the fulcrum is placed to the object being raised, the less force is required to lift it.

Examples of simple tools that use the lever principle include scissors, tongs, pliers, pump handles, seesaws, nail pullers, and nutcrackers. In the latter case, the fulcrum can be situated at one end rather than in the middle.

The **catapult** or **ballista**, an ancient weapon of war used for hurling large objects, is also based on the lever.

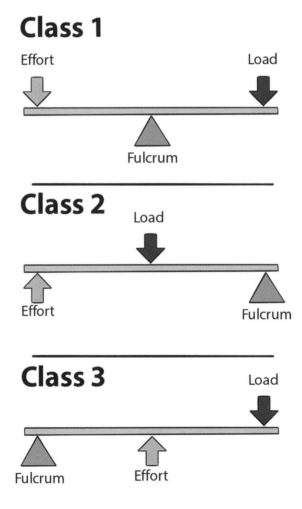

Class 1
Effort Load
Fulcrum

Class 2
Load
Effort Fulcrum

Class 3
Load
Fulcrum Effort

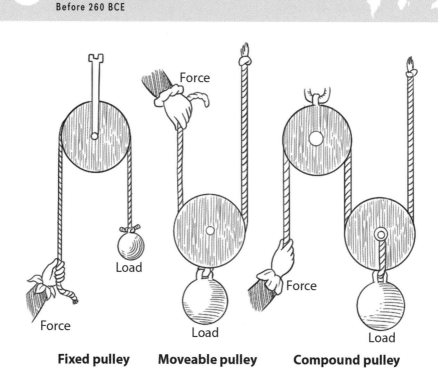

Force

Load

Force

Force

Load

Force

Load

Fixed pulley   **Moveable pulley**   **Compound pulley**

The **pulley** is one of the **six simple machines**. Based on the wheel, it was first described by the Greek scientist and engineer Archimedes. The **compound pulley** and the **block and tackle** were developed later.

The pulley uses a wheel with its rim grooved to provide a path for a cable or a rope, by which a person or a motor can then hoist a heavy object. The wheel is used to change the direction of the force being exerted. For example, an elevator is raised by a motor that pulls down a cable looped over a pulley at the top of the elevator shaft. The compound pulley can multiply the hoisting power of a person or a motor, but it requires a longer pulling distance.

A group of pulleys mounted in parallel can further increase lifting power. A basic principle of pulleys holds that their lifting power is multiplied by the number of strands acting directly upon the moving pulleys.

In a block and tackle rigging system, many individual pulleys are combined into blocks for increased lifting power.

The concept of the **spiral screw** is attributed to the Greek mathematician and inventor Archimedes. A spiral screw is an inclined plane wrapped around a cylinder. The spiral is commonly known as the **thread**, and the distance between adjacent edges of the spiral along the axis of the cylinder is called the **pitch** of the screw. The pitch is equal to the distance that the screw advances in one turn while penetrating a solid medium.

Archimedes reputedly devised the screw as a rotating pump to raise water from streams into irrigation ditches. The **Archimedean screw** was immersed in a water source at a shallow angle so that the lowest part of any given thread was lower than the highest part of the thread below it. When the shaft of the screw was rotated on its axis so that the threads screwed into the water, water was lifted up the spiral and discharged from the top of the thread.

Fastening devices are among the most familiar applications of the spiral screw. A **wood screw** is a tapered, pointed, metal spiral that creates a very tight hold thanks to its wedge-shaped thread that forces the wood fibers apart as it rotates into a slightly undersized hole. The **machine screw** is a fastener of constant diameter that can be made any length and can engage a negative, or **female, thread** formed around the inside of a hole in a free-turning **nut** or piece of material.

The spiral is also used in **augers** and **twist drills**, which are used for boring holes in materials. To drill a hole, the drill or **bit** is rotated until the spiral thread advances into the material. In these tools, the pitch is usually long in relation to the diameter of the drill. The wide spiral edges of a drill are called **lands**, and the smooth grooves between them that lift away the waste material removed from the hole like the water in an Archimedean screw are called **flutes**. Augers and drills appear in Western European paintings as early as 1425 CE.

Drills are often mounted in simple rotating machines. The **brace** and the **hand drill** are drilling machines that have changed very little throughout their long history and are still used in many parts of the world. The **power drill** became a necessity to produce heavy machinery during the Industrial Revolution of the eighteenth century. French engineer Jacques de Vaucanson built a powered **drill press** in 1728, and the first **handheld power drill**, driven by clockwork, was introduced in England in 1864. Finally, an **electric hand drill** was invented in Germany by Wilhelm Fein in 1895.

The spiral screw has been made in all sizes. Huge augers—some as large in diameter as the height of a man—are used to remove borings from mines and tunnels, and steel screws—some so small they can barely be seen with the unaided eye—are used in fine Swiss watches. A thimbleful of a thousand such screws costs more than their weight in gold!

Humans had been grinding grain into flour by hand for thousands of years before the power of a running stream was harnessed into the circular motion of a **waterwheel** to do the task. A water wheel is a partially submerged wheel with paddles, and it turns when water runs against or drops onto the paddles. This automated system made it possible for a higher volume of grain to be processed much more quickly. The first water-powered mills were built over streams, with the wheels mounted horizontally under the mill. An axle came through the floor and was connected to a flat millstone.

The waterwheel probably originated in the Middle East but was soon adopted by the Greeks and later the Europeans. This technology was used for jobs other than grinding grain, too, such as sawing wood and processing cloth.

The use of the waterwheel principle to produce electricity was devised in 1891 in Germany. In **hydroelectric power**, a large volume of water is stored behind a dam to guarantee an adequate supply at a controllable flow rate. This water is released through a **turbine** to generate electricity.

A modern turbine is essentially a highly developed waterwheel that transforms the kinetic energy of moving water into mechanical energy at the hub of its wheel, thus generating electricity.

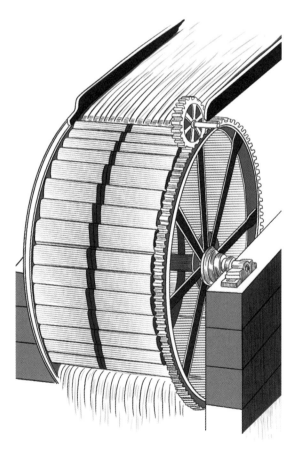

The **magnetic compass,** a device used to locate a northerly direction and aid navigation, is essentially a magnetized needle suspended in a box so that it can pivot freely. The needle aligns with the north–south axis of the magnetic field of the Earth.

The discovery that a magnetic needle always aligns north–south occurred in China and is described in writings of Wang Xu. By the ninth century, Chinese scientists had developed both the **floating needle** and **pivoting needle** compasses that we know today. Persian sailors acquired some of these compasses, and in turn, traded some with Venetian merchants soon after.

In 1187, English writer Alexander Neckam described a "pointer carried on board [a ship] which enables a course to be followed even when the Polar star is hidden by clouds."

The **gyrocompass** was invented in Germany in 1908 and was adapted by Elmer Ambrose Sperry for use in aircrafts and ships. This remarkable instrument uses the angular momentum of a **gyroscope** with the force produced by the Earth's rotation to maintain a north–south orientation of the spin axis, thus providing a stable directional reference.

Grain was ground into flour by hand for many centuries before the first waterwheel-powered mills were built in the first century BCE. Amazingly, it would be almost another thousand years before millers harnessed the power of wind for a helpful purpose. A windmill is like a waterwheel (see no. 16) except that it uses the kinetic energy of moving air rather than flowing water against paddles to turn a cylindrical shaft and power a grinding wheel.

The development of the **windmill** was a matter of geography. Some areas had fast-running streams available while others did not. In locales that were particularly windy, people learned they could harness the power of the wind to operate their mills. This concept is thought to have evolved in the Middle East and was later adopted by the Greeks and other societies in the Mediterranean region.

Windmills became very important to the economy of Northern Europe where gusts from the North Sea are particularly intense. Windmills of sixteenth- and seventeenth-century design are still a familiar sight in Belgium, Germany, and especially in the Netherlands. Across the plains of the United States and Canada, windmills were still used to pump water from farms well into the twentieth century.

The use of windmills to generate electrical power first occurred in the United States in 1876 and was subsequently used throughout the world. After the worldwide oil crisis of the 1970s, interest in the use of wind power to produce electricity increased and many utility companies invested in wind generation projects. A huge **"wind farm"** at Altamont Pass near San Francisco contains hundreds of high technology windmills that generate about 4 percent of the electrical energy for the Northern California power grid.

Early Christian clerics created sanctuaries called "hospitia" that were modeled after the Roman *valetudinaria*. In these havens, monks and nuns nursed, fed, and clothed the unfortunate. Leprosaria and permanent homes for the old, sick, and poor were established along similar lines. Although most of these hospices offered nursing care, there was no medical aid. In effect, these institutions were nursing homes and hospitals without doctors. The modern **hospital** has its true origin in the monastic infirmaries of the Middle Ages. In 822 CE, Abbot Rabanus Maurus drew up the blueprints for an abbey at the monastic school of Fulda in Germany, and added a special wing for sick brothers, a lazaretto for those with contagious diseases, and an apartment for a monastic doctor. Abbot Gozbert did likewise while building the monastery of St. Galle in Switzerland, and soon the procedure became standard. Gozbert also mapped out what became the traditional medicinal garden outside the hospital. Sick and needy laypeople came to the monastic infirmaries and physicians for medical aid in increasing numbers, and these religious institutions became the forerunners of the modern hospital.

The science of telling the time of day, or **horology**, began around 3500 BCE with the invention of the **gnomon** and the **sundial** (see no. 8). These inventions worked well in the daytime when the Sun shone but were useless at night. The **hourglass**, invented during the same period, uses a fixed quantity of fine sand or other granular material that falls through a narrow opening to measure a specific elapsed interval of time, but not the time of day. The Egyptian **clepsydra**, or **water clock**, invented circa 1500 BCE, was a form of hourglass that used water dripping between two marked containers to indicate the passage of time. For instance, if it took twenty-four hours for the water to drip from one to the other and the process began at noon, then two half-full containers indicated midnight. Variations on the clepsydra were widely used in Greece, Rome, and elsewhere, but they were never very accurate because shifts in temperature, weight, and water pressure affected the frequency of the drips. The most advanced precursor to the mechanical clock was developed in China in 725 CE by a monk named Yi Xing.

The first **mechanical clock** is attributed to French Benedictine monk Gerbert d'Aurillac, who became Pope Sylvester II in 999 CE. Gerbert's design used a system of gears run by counterbalanced weights. The first mention of a clock that struck a bell on the hour was recorded in Citeaux, France, in 1120. Early mechanical clocks were all large, fixed devices. The portable, **spring-driven clock** appears to have been invented in Florence, Italy, in 1410 by the famed architect Filippo Brunelleschi. The invention of the **pendulum clock** dates to 1657 and is attributed to the Dutch inventor and astronomer Christian Huygens. Huygens discovered the near-constant frequency of oscillation of the pendulum and adapted it to improve the accuracy of mechanical clocks. The first **electric clocks** appeared in 1840 as a result of the work of the Scottish inventor Alexander Bain. What is perhaps the first **spring-driven alarm clock** of the familiar modern type was built in France in 1847 by clockmaker Antoine Redier. The first **electric alarm clock** was introduced around 1890.

Pocket watches evolved after the fifteenth century as miniaturizations of portable clocks, and the self-winding watch was invented by the French clockmaker A. L. Perrelet. The first **wristwatch** is said to have been made by Louis-Francois Cartier of France for his friend and Brazilian aviator Alberto Santos-Dumont to confirm a speed record on November 27, 1907. The first **self-winding watches** appeared in 1924, and the first **waterproof watch** was developed by Rolex brand founder Hans Wilsdorf in 1926.

The Chinese had been interested in explosive devices since about 300 BCE when they heated bamboo to cause an explosion, but their invention of **gunpowder** opened the door to a whole world of destructive inventions. A good deal of conscious experimentation probably went into the ultimate discovery that a mixture of charcoal, saltpeter, and sulfur would explode when it came in contact with fire.

Gunpowder, or **black powder**, was invented around the year 1040 CE. It was first used in fireworks but was soon adapted for military purposes, such as the launching of small rockets. The Chinese military used it in bombs and cannons during the thirteenth century, and it was used in wars in the Middle East not long after. In fact, gunpowder was first used to launch projectiles from a portable gun the size of a modern rifle in Arabia in 1304 (see no. 25). The use of gunpowder—first as an explosive and later in firearms—amplified many times over the destructive power of weapons and revolutionized warfare.

Gunpowder was also used as an industrial explosive for nearly eight hundred years until it was superseded by an even more powerful substance. In 1846, Ascanio Sobrero, an Italian chemist, invented **nitroglycerin**, a chemical mixture of two-to-one ratio of **sulfuric acid** and **nitric acid**, which proved to be many times more potent by weight than gunpowder and much more dangerous. In 1862, nitroglycerin was adapted by Alfred Nobel in Sweden as a practical explosive for use in civil engineering (see no. 49).

Today, gunpowder continues to be used primarily in the launch of projectiles from guns. A major milestone in the history of gunpowder occurred in 1884 when Paul Vieille in France developed smokeless gunpowder. Prior to this time, when a shot was fired by a gun, the explosion of gunpowder would emit a puff of smoke. In wartime, this meant that a soldier risked revealing their position by firing their gun. Thus, the development of **smokeless gunpowder** was a welcome innovation. Vieille created the new gunpowder by dissolving **nitrocellulose** in **ether** or **alcohol** to create a sludge that, when dried, exploded without producing smoke. Another advantage of the new smokeless powder was that it left less residue in a gun barrel than conventional black powder.

Printing is the process of making multiple copies of a document by using movable characters or letters. The process was developed independently in China and Europe. Before the invention of printing, multiple copies of a manuscript had to be made by hand, a laborious task that could take many years. Printing made it possible to produce more copies in a few weeks than what was once produced in a lifetime by hand.

Bi Sheng (Pi Cheng) in China is generally recognized as the man who invented printing. In 1041, he printed his first documents using letters, which he had baked in clay and assembled into sentences that were locked into a frame. Bi Zheng's process was improved by Wang Zhen in 1298, who made his characters out of hardwood and went on to print books and even newspapers. As European trade with China expanded and flourished over the next several centuries, the printing process became known in the West. In 1423, Dutch inventor Laurens Janszoon Coster experimented with printing in the Roman alphabet using metal characters to produce a clay printing plate.

These methods were a great improvement over hand-copying, but they were still unwieldy. In about 1436, a German inventor named Johannes Gutenberg began his work on a machine—the **printing press**—that would make printing a much faster and more economical procedure. He adapted, or reinvented, Bi Sheng's idea of **movable type**; that is, the idea that hundreds of individual letters could be combined in numerous ways to lay out an entire page.

Gutenberg used his printing press to put ink on the letter blocks and printed as many copies as he desired. He then disassembled the first page and recombined the letter blocks for subsequent pages until the entire document was complete. Among Gutenberg's greatest achievements was the first mass-produced edition of the Bible, which he published in Mainz, Germany, around 1456.

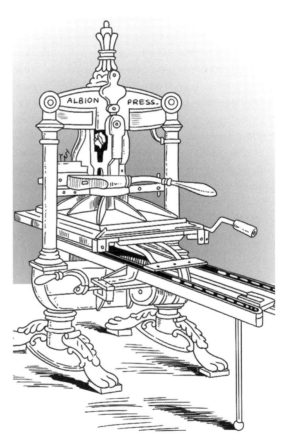

A **rocket** is a means of thrusting forward a projectile or vehicle by the force of fuel that is being burned in a combustion chamber and ejected from a nozzle in the rear of the object being propelled. In contemporary usage, a **rocket engine** differs from a **jet engine** in that rockets carry their own oxygen and jets rely on the intake of surrounding air. Jets are more easily controlled, but rockets are faster and can operate in an airless environment, such as outer space.

There are two types of rockets based on two different fuels: solid and liquid. The first **solid-fuel rockets** were projectiles powered by exploding gunpowder, and these were used as fireworks and weapons in China as early as 1232. The British navy used rockets developed by ballistics engineer William Congreve to bombard targets on shore during the Napoleonic Wars and the War of 1812. Congreve used launching tubes to improve the accuracy of his rockets.

American physicist Robert H. Goddard launched the first **liquid-fuel** rocket on March 16, 1926, and by the late 1930s, many theorists were suggesting that rockets might be the key to practical human travel in outer space. The first large, long-range rockets were the **V-2 (A-4)** missiles designed by Wernher von Braun and built in Germany in World War II to bombard England from deep inside Germany.

Von Braun had always been interested in space travel, and after World War II, he emigrated to the United States, where he played a key role in the American space program. At the same time, many of his colleagues went to the USSR to work for the Soviet space program. It can be said that all major rocket programs in both countries well into the 1960s and 1970s were direct descendants of Wernher von Braun's V-2 missile.

The largest rocket ever built was the 363-foot-tall **Saturn 5**, whose liquid-fueled engines could deliver 8.8 million pounds of thrust. Saturn 5s were used between 1969 and 1972 to send American astronauts to the moon. The last one was used in 1973 to launch the Skylab Space Station. The largest rocket vehicle in use until 2011, the **American Space Shuttle**, employed a combination of liquid- and cheaper solid-fuel rockets to deliver 6.7 million pounds of thrust.

Robert Goddard with his first liquid-fuel rocket before its launch

Glass lenses, for use as magnifiers or for starting fires, date to about 300 BCE, but the first **eyeglasses** to aid or correct vision were almost certainly invented in 1280 in Florence, Italy, by either Dominican friar Alessandro della Spina or his friend, physicist Salvino degli Armati. Prescribed for **hypermetropia**, or farsightedness, the glasses had convex lenses and were worn by Armati, who had injured his eyes while performing light refraction experiments and discovered that it was possible to enlarge the appearance of objects by looking through two pieces of convex glass.

It was in the early fourteenth century that concave lenses were used to correct **myopia**, or nearsightedness. In fact, Pope Leo X was depicted wearing glasses with concave lenses in a 1517 painting by Raphael. Whereas early eyeglasses were made of polished quartz, by the sixteenth century, developments in glassmaking made it possible to mass-produce them from glass.

Framed glasses, as we know them today, were apparently introduced in 1746 by French optical firm Thomin.

Bifocals, the combination of both concave and convex lenses for both types of vision correction, incorporated a top lens for distant viewing and a lower lens for reading. These were developed around 1784 by American statesman and inventor Benjamin Franklin.

If we define a **gun** as "a tube through which a projectile is fired," then the primitive **blow gun**—the type still used by indigenous peoples in the Amazon River basin—would qualify. In 245 BCE, Greek engineer Ctesibius devised a **compressed air** blow gun, which consisted of a bronze tube fitted with a piston that could fire arrows.

In 1040, **gunpowder** (see no. 21) was invented in China. It was used in fireworks and as an industrial explosive. As noted earlier, gunpowder was first used in Arabia in 1304 to launch projectiles from a portable gun the size of a modern rifle.

Artillery, or large guns, differ from small arms like rifles and pistols. These include cannons, howitzers, and mortars. Chinese **cannons** first appeared in the thirteenth century and are known to have been used in the defeat of a Mongol fleet off the coast of Japan in 1281. After this, naval cannons were used on European ships beginning in 1346. They were designed to fire in as straight as possible at a visible target. The **howitzer** was developed in the seventeenth century in the English and Dutch armies to fire explosive shells in a high arc to hit a distant target, often one that is beyond the line of sight.

The **mortar** is an extrapolation of the howitzer idea that evolved in its present form during World War I. A mortar fires its projectile at a very steep trajectory so that when it reaches the target, it has actually fallen from a great height and, hence, has added velocity due to its fall.

Artillery was originally **muzzle-loaded**, meaning that the projectile was dropped or pushed into the front opening of the gun barrel. Since the late nineteenth century, artillery has been typically **breech-loaded**, meaning that it is put into a **firing chamber** at the opposite end of the gun from the muzzle. Mortars, however, are still muzzle-loaded.

A Chinese cannon

Although large guns emerged in the thirteenth century, neither the compressed air nor gunpowder system was usually considered practical or accurate enough for small arms.

The **arquebus**, the first true ancestor of the modern rifle, first emerged in Spain around 1450 and was employed with great success in the Spanish defeat of the French at Cerignola, Italy, in 1503. In 1570, the **flintlock musket**, in which the powder was ignited by the action of flint on metal, replaced the arquebus. Like its predecessor, the musket was muzzle-loaded. This system remained the standard for both rifles and pistols for the next two hundred years.

In 1845, the first functional **metal cartridge**, such as those in use today, was invented in France. With this refinement, it was possible to load a small arm at the breech rather than at the muzzle. However, in most cases, projectiles could still only be fired one at a time until the invention of the **repeater** (see no. 42 and no. 48).

The **harpsichord** and **piano** are both derived from **stringed musical instruments** like the harp (see no. 10). Unlike the harp or guitar, however, the strings in a harpsichord and a piano are not played directly but rather mechanically via a keyboard. The difference between the two instruments is that the harpsichord's strings are plucked while a piano's keys are struck. Members of the harpsichord family include the **virginal, psaltery,** and **spinet**, while the **clavichord** is more similar to the piano.

The harpsichord was preceded by the **monochord**, which was invented in Greece in about 220 BCE by Archimedes. The harpsichord in its present form originated in the fourteenth century, although the name was first used in 1631.

The related spinet was invented by Giovanni Spinetti in Venice in 1530. The piano is based on an idea that can be traced to ancient Greece. Guido d'Arezzo is mentioned as having built a similar instrument in the eleventh century. The clavichord dates to the end of the fourteenth century and is depicted in German drawings from that period.

The invention of the modern piano occurred in Tuscany in present-day Italy and is credited to Bortolmeo Cristofori, who developed the instrument between 1698 and 1720. The original name was **pianoforte**, which is derived from the Italian words *piano* meaning "soft" and *forte* meaning "loud," indicating that the instrument had the means to control the volume of its sounded notes, and as such, it was more melodious than its predecessors.

The **grand piano**, with highly tensioned strings and a large soundboard, was introduced in 1853 by the German-born American piano builder Heinrich Engelhard Steinweg. He anglicized his surname to Steinway and founded the famous Steinway piano company.

The use of concave and convex glass lenses to increase the apparent size of objects revolutionized science because it was finally possible to see things that had been too tiny or too distant to be discerned by the naked eye. Both the **microscope** and the **telescope** (see no. 28) were products of this revolution. The microscope, a device for viewing very small, minute objects, probably came first as a direct evolution of the lens used for **eyeglasses** (see no. 24). In 1590, Zacharias Janssen and his father made the first microscope in the Netherlands, although the first focusing mechanism for the microscope was developed in 1668 by Campini, a scientist in Italy.

Another Dutch scientist and microscope builder, Antonie van Leeuwenhoek, was the first to use the microscope to study bacteria in 1660. His microscopes, which had magnifying powers up to 270, were considered by many to be the best available at the time for studying **microorganisms** and human blood cells.

The theoretical grounds for the **electron microscope**, a device used to observe objects as small as one-millionth of a millimeter by using the wave properties of electrons, was pioneered in Germany by Hans Busch in 1926. Busch's work was later elaborated upon by Ernst Ruska and Max Knoll at the Technische Hochschule in Berlin, where they constructed the first practical electron microscope in 1933.

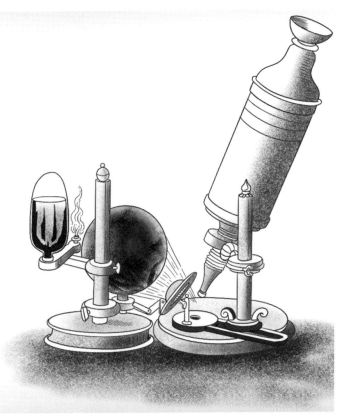

The use of concave and convex glass lenses to aid the eye was of vital importance to the advancement of the sciences. The invention of the **microscope** (see no. 27), a device for viewing small objects, preceded by only a few years the invention of the **telescope**, an instrument for observing distant objects. Both were created in the Netherlands.

Hans Lippershey of Middleburg is credited with the invention of the telescope around 1608. However, it was the renowned Italian astronomer Galileo Galilei who first revealed the telescope's full potential. Based on Lippershey's model, he constructed his first telescope in 1609 and turned it toward the planets, becoming the first to see them as spherical bodies—as places rather than merely glowing objects in the night sky. In 1610, Galileo discovered the four largest moons of Jupiter—the first moons ever observed around a planet other than Earth—and the rings of Saturn. As he continued his observation of the heavens, he became the first to view mountains on the Moon and spots on the Sun. Unfortunately, his study of sunspots eventually rendered him blind.

The Galilean telescope was of a simple design, with two refracting lenses arranged between the object and the viewer's eye. In 1670, the English scientist and astronomer Sir Isaac Newton, perhaps the greatest physicist to live prior to the twentieth century, invented the **reflecting telescope**. His instrument used a concave mirror to reflect the image to be viewed onto a flat plate or eyepiece and could resolve fainter or more distant astronomic objects than earlier refracting telescopes.

The **radio telescope** is a twentieth-century development that is distinct from the previously described **optical telescopes**. Radio astronomy, which involves the study of radio waves that originate in deep space, was first undertaken by Karl Guthe Jansky of the Bell Telephone Laboratories in the United States after he accidentally discovered that discrete frequencies of radio waves were emanating from distant stars and galaxies. These waves emit light waves of the visible spectrum, and stars and galaxies also send out identifiable spectra of radio waves. The first major permanent radio telescope was built in 1957 at Jodrell Bank in England.

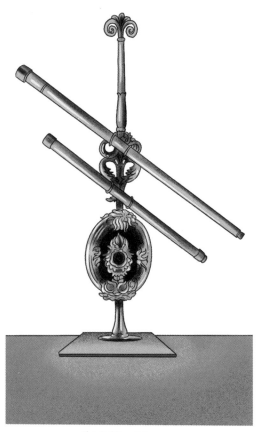

The Galilean telescope

The **submarine** is, by definition, a boat that can travel under the surface of the water. Until recently, submarines had little use except in warfare and underwater research because surface ships have been far more economical than a craft that must be entirely watertight and carry an artificial source of air for its crew. In warfare, however, the submarine is a very potent weapon as it can attack its targets without being seen. In the U.S. Navy, there is a saying that there are only two kinds of warships: submarines and targets. During both world wars, German submarines were very effective in the North Atlantic, as were U.S. Navy subs in the blockade of Japan in World War II.

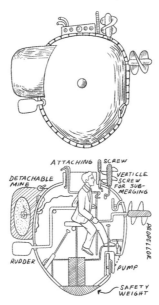

Bushnell's *Turtle*

Although practical submarines did not appear until World War I, the basic concept dates back to Leonardo da Vinci—or even before that—and the actual invention of the submarine took place around 1624. Cornelius Drebbel, a Dutch inventor and engineer employed by the British Navy, constructed a leather-covered submersible rowboat from which oars protruded through watertight seals. Based on a design reportedly drawn in 1573 by Queen Elizabeth's naval gunnery chief, William Bourne, Drebbel's ship traveled 15 feet beneath the surface and could stay down for several hours. Numerous other submarines were built in England and America in the eighteenth century.

The first use of a submarine as a weapon of war occurred in 1776, when the submarine *Turtle*, designed by a Connecticut engineer named David Bushnell, was used to assault the British frigate *Eagle* in the New York Harbor. The *Turtle*, an egg-shaped vessel about 10 feet (3 meters) high powered by hand-cranked screws, had as its offensive weapon a drill that was to be used to make a hole in the bottom of the *Eagle*'s hull. Although this tactic failed, the *Turtle* pointed the way to the future use of submarines.

Over the next century, more submarines were built in Europe and America, and the first successful sinking of a surface ship by a submarine was recorded during the American Civil War. The Confederate submarine *David* (one of several with the same name) sank the Union frigate *Housatonic* outside Charleston Harbor on February 17, 1864, but the vessel was lost.

In the wake of German **diesel submarine** (*Unterseeboots* or "U-boats") success in World War I, submarines became a standard warship in all modern navies. The most important development in submarine technology in the twentieth century was the adaptation of small nuclear reactors for use as power plants. The first such vessel was the USS *Nautilus* (SSN-571) that launched on January 17, 1955. **Nuclear submarines**, which today form the backbone of the undersea fleets of the American, Russian, British, and other navies, are quieter than diesel-powered subs, can remain submerged for much longer periods of time, and have a virtually limitless range.

Humans had used controlled fire to modify their environment for thousands of centuries before means were discovered to activate fires chemically. At some time long before the beginning of recorded history, people in widely separated parts of the world learned how to spark fires at first by the friction of rubbing two sticks together, and later (and more easily), with flint and steel. However, it was not until 1680 that Robert Boyle of England discovered that phosphorus and sulfur would burst into flame instantly if rubbed together. He was convinced that the flames were caused not by friction but by something inherent in the two elements. He was right. He had uncovered the principal that would ultimately lead to the modern **match**. Then, in the early nineteenth century, many different chemical fire-starting devices were developed in Europe. Some used Boyle's phosphorus/sulfur combination while others involved gaseous hydrogen, but all were quite cumbersome and dangerous.

In 1827, an English pharmacist named John Walker produced his "sulphuretted peroxide strikables"—gigantic, yard-long sticks that could be considered the real precursor of today's match. Small phosphorus matches were first marketed in Germany in 1832, but they were extremely hazardous. This problem was not resolved until the invention of amorphous (red) phosphorus in 1845. Carl Lundström of Sweden introduced the first red phosphorus "safety" matches in 1855.

The **liquid thermometer** is based on the principle that liquid expands or contracts with changes in temperature and thus will rise or fall in a closed tube. If the change in volume is proportional to the temperature change, a liquid-filled glass or other transparent tube can be calibrated to determine specific temperatures.

The first instrument for identifying specific temperatures was reputedly made by Philo of Byzantium around 200 BCE and reinvented by Ctesibius of Alexandria about 100 years later. Ctesibius' invention was a glass tube shaped like an inverted "U" with a container at each end. When the liquid in one container was heated, it rose due to expansion. This system was either copied or reinvented in 1593 by the great Italian scientist Galileo Galilei.

The first **alcohol thermometer** was made in 1654 for Archduke Ferdinand II of Tuscany by an enameller named Mariani. The familiar **mercury thermometer** was created in 1714 by Gabriel Daniel Fahrenheit, a native of Danzig (also known as Gdańsk in Polish) who did most of his work in Holland and England. He chose mercury, the only liquid metal, because of its very low freezing temperature (–37.8°F) and very high boiling point (675°F). This meant that a drastic variation in temperature could be contained in a relatively compact tube. His thermometers were an immediate commercial success as they provided the first practical means of accurately calibrating temperature. He also devised the **Fahrenheit system** of measuring temperatures, in which water freezes at 32°F and boils at 212°F. Although this system was promptly adopted for use in England and is still in use in the United States today, it was later superseded by the Celsius system in most of the world.

The **Celsius system** is also known as the **centigrade system** because it uses a 100-degree interval between the freezing temperature (0°C) and the boiling point (100°C) of water. This system was introduced in 1741 by the Swedish thermometer maker Anders Celsius. Adopted in France in 1795, it is now the world standard.

The first use of a mercury thermometer by a physician to determine the temperature of a human is attributed to Sir Thomas Allbutt in 1866.

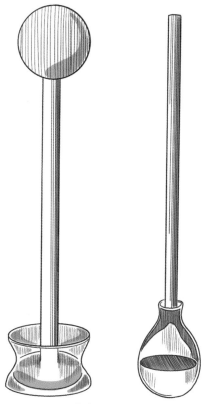

Early thermometers

The idea of the **steam engine** was first explored by Heron of Alexandria (second century CE), who observed that the expansion of water vapor could be harnessed to provide energy for making an object move or turn. He built a machine called the **aeolipile**, or "wind ball," which was a sphere with two spouts that rotated on a hollow axle connected to a boiler. Technically, Heron's aeolipile was a true steam engine, but apparently no one could envision a practical application for it, and the concept was abandoned for over a thousand years. The Marquis of Worcester in 1640, Denis Papin in 1687, and Thomas Savery in 1698 each built simple steam devices that used the expansion of water vapor to provide energy. However, like Heron had experienced many centuries prior, their steam machines were too slow and inconsistent in their performance to be anything but curiosities.

The first practical steam engine—one that could not only run but also run another machine—was the brainchild of James E. Watt. Watt, a Scottish engineer, studied earlier machines and made numerous changes, including adding insulation around the boiler to prevent heat loss and converting the linear thrust of the steam piston to the circular motion of a drive shaft.

His first steam engine, completed in 1769, was much more efficient than any previous effort, but it was not until 1774 that he was able to call his invention a practical success. It was quickly put into use for power factory equipment, such as lathes and spinning machines.

Large-scale applications of steam power, such as locomotives and steam ships, would not appear until the next century. These inventions were products of the Industrial Revolution, one of the few events that truly altered the course of human history. The Industrial Revolution was an amalgam of ideas about machines and their potential for expanding the physical power of humankind, whether it was the power to manufacture goods or the power to move quickly over the surface of the Earth. There was a flood of ideas and inventions at the dawn of the **Industrial Revolution**, but few would have been possible without the machine that provided power: the steam engine.

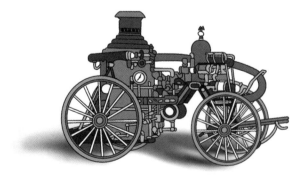

Since the dawn of time, humans have been intrigued by the mystery of flight and the apparent magic that allows birds to take to the air and soar for hours. Attempts to copy birds by building wings that could be flapped by attaching them to the arms failed consistently through the years, and it wasn't until these methods were abandoned that ultimate success was achieved.

In 1766 in England, Henry Cavendish isolated hydrogen, the simplest of elements and the lightest of gases. Since it was lighter than air, he described it as having "negative weight" and proposed that it could be used to lift objects from the Earth, but he apparently never pursued the idea. In 1782 in France, Joseph-Michel Montgolfier filled a silk bag with hot air, which being less dense than the air around it, lifted the bag to the high ceiling of his house. On April 25, 1783, he and his brother Jacques-Étienne built a larger spherical bag, filled it with hot air from a fire, and sent several farm animals aloft in a basket hung beneath it.

After this success, they created an even larger envelope, and on November 21, 1783, in the Bois de Boulogne in Paris, the brothers launched a 70-foot-high balloon carrying Jean-François Pilâtre de Rozier and the Marquis d'Arlandes. The two men were lifted to 3,000 feet, becoming the first humans to experience sustained flight. They remained aloft for 25 minutes and traveled 5 miles, controlling their own flight by adding straw to the fire. When this accomplishment was widely publicized, the human-carrying balloon evolved quickly. On December 1, 1783, in Paris, Jacques Charles and Noel Roberts flew 27 miles in the first flight of a hydrogen-filled balloon. Elizabeth Thible, the first woman to fly in a balloon, went aloft at Lyon, France, on June 4, 1784. The first British-designed balloon was flown by its builder, James Satler, on October 4, 1784, and the first balloon flight in the United States was conducted by French citizen Jean-Pierre Blanchard of Philadelphia on January 9, 1793. Blanchard and the American Dr. John Jeffries had been the first humans to fly across the English Channel, on January 7, 1785. (In that same year, Blanchard invented and first used the **parachute**.)

The French army formed the world's first "air force" when they used balloons to observe the opposing Austrian forces during the Battle of Fleurus on June 26, 1794.

Mithridates Eupator, King of Pontus, who ruled from 120–63 BCE, unwittingly helped to establish the principle of **immunology**. The king lived in perpetual fear that his foes would poison him. Anxious to discover a substance to counteract their deadly potions, he tested poisonous drugs on criminals, and then ingested some of these substances himself in slowly increasing quantities. He found that taken in this way, they had no ill effect. Thus, Mithridates, because of his experiments, is regarded as the world's first immunologist.

Developed in regions from China to Turkey in response to the smallpox epidemic of the eighteenth century, **vaccination** was first used in the West by Zabdiel Boylston of Boston, Massachusetts, in June 1721. George Washington first had his household and then his army inoculated. Benjamin Franklin also became an advocate of the idea after smallpox killed his youngest son.

Edward Jenner, a busy country doctor in Gloucestershire, was the first to conduct a series of experiments to test the relationship between smallpox and cowpox. After twenty-eight years of observation, Jenner found that liquid of the pustules taken from a patient suffering from cowpox (*vaccinia*) had the power to protect others from smallpox (*variola*). After he had checked all his observations carefully, he undertook the experiment that made him immortal in the annals of medicine.

On May 14, 1796, Jenner vaccinated the arm of a boy, John James Phipps, with the lymph taken from a cowpox pustule on the infected hand of the dairymaid, Sarah Nelmes. Then, six weeks later, young Phipps was inoculated with smallpox. No trace of infection appeared. Further tests proved conclusively that the vaccination acted as an effective, easily applied means of preventing smallpox.

Amazingly, Jenner's important first paper on his vaccination experiments received only a rejection slip from the Royal Society of Medicine. The Society held that the paper's contents would spoil the good name that he had gained by his previous research on the cuckoo bird. Jenner finally earned worldwide attention when he published his findings in 1798. His experiments provided the foundation for the art of preventive medicine, which was born in the nineteenth century (see no. 71).

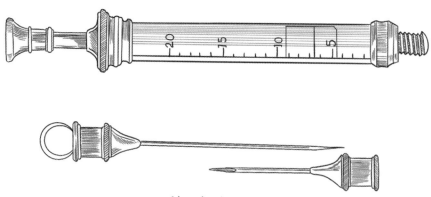

A hypodermic syringe

Electricity has fascinated humankind since our ancestors first witnessed lightning. In ancient Greece, Thales observed that an electric charge could be generated by rubbing amber, for which the Greek word is *elektron*. German physicist Otto von Guericke experimented with generating electricity in 1650, English physicist Stephen Gray discovered electrical conductivity in 1729, and American statesman and inventor Benjamin Franklin studied the properties of electricity by conducting his famous experiment of flying a kite with a key attached to it during storms.

However, the first workable device for generating a consistent flow of electricity was invented around 1800 by the Italian inventor Alessandro Volta. Volta's discovery of a means of converting chemical energy into electrical energy formed the basis for nearly all modern batteries.

Beginning his work in the 1770s, Volta observed the electrical interaction between two different metals submerged near each other in an acidic solution. Based on this principle, his first battery consisted of a series of alternating copper and zinc rings in an acid solution known as an **electrolyte**. He called his invention a **column battery**, although it came to be commonly known as the **Volta battery** or **Voltaic cell**. The term **volt**, a unit for measuring electrical potential difference and electromotive force, is also derived from his name.

The next step in the evolution of electrical energy storage was the invention of the **lead acid storage battery** in 1859 by French physicist Gaston Planté. This chemical battery used a liquid electrolyte and was not easy to move. This situation changed with the development of the **dry cell battery**, which was based on the pioneering work done between 1867 and 1877 by Georges Leclanché in France. In the dry cell battery, the electrolyte is a damp paste so that there is no liquid to leak out, making it quite portable.

The **alkaline storage battery** is in common use today, and it was developed in 1914 by Thomas Edison. It is so called because the electrolyte is alkaline, or basic, rather than acidic. Like the electrolyte in a dry cell, it is not a liquid, so it can be easily transported.

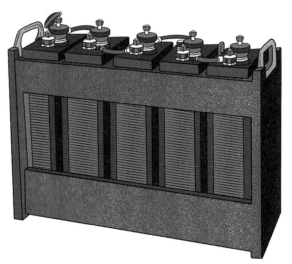

Five battery cells

For over a century, **steam locomotives** were by far the most important mechanized land vehicle. The first steam-powered vehicle was built in 1769 by Nicolas-Joseph Cugnot. It was a steam road tractor that appeared only four years after James Watt had built a practical steam engine (see no. 32). However, Cugnot's invention was a slow and ponderous machine, and as such, was deemed impractical.

The first locomotive to run on rails was the steam carriage built in 1803 by Richard Trevithick at Coalbrookdale in Wales. He tested his new machine on February 2, 1804, by running it over a nine-mile track with passengers on board. The next two milestones in the development of the locomotive both occurred in England. The first mass-produced locomotives were introduced in 1812 by John Blenkinsop, and the first high-speed locomotive, the Rocket, was built in 1829 by Robert Stephenson and his father, George. The Rocket was capable of speeds up to 16 miles per hour while pulling a 40-ton train or 36 miles per hour without a load. It was the first man-made land vehicle that could outrun a horse. The first **passenger locomotive**, built in 1829 by Peter Cooper in the United States for the Baltimore & Ohio Railroad, was the Tom Thumb.

The Mallet **articulated compound locomotive** was introduced in Europe in 1887 and in the United States in 1904. It used two sets of driving wheels propelled by two independent steam engines, and the boiler pivoted on the chassis. The power of steam locomotives was determined by their size, and their length was restricted by the curves in the track over which they ran. Articulation permitted the locomotive to be longer because it could pivot around curves.

The first **electric locomotives** appeared in service on a branch of the New Haven & Hartford Railroad in the United States on June 28, 1895. The first main line electric locomotive service began just five weeks later on the Baltimore & Ohio.

Diesel locomotives were first built in Switzerland in 1912 but were initially deemed less efficient than their steam-powered cousins. The first practical streamlined diesel was the German Flying Hamburger, which started operation in May 1932. In the United States, the diesel streamliner Pioneer Zephyr made a 1,015-mile nonstop run on the Chicagoan Burlington & Quincy Railroad between Denver and Chicago, averaging 77.6 miles per hour, on May 26, 1934. By the late 1930s, diesel locomotives began replacing steam on most major passenger routes in North America, and by the mid-1950s they were the leading means of motive power on American railroads, although they were far outnumbered by electric locomotives in Europe.

The idea of using steam power to propel a boat dates back to 1685 and the writings of French citizen Denis Papin, but Papin never actually finished building his twin-paddle wheel machine. In 1730, English inventor Jonathan Hulls powered a rowboat with a steam pump that turned a crank attached to a paddle wheel. Although his invention ran, it was erratic and consumed too much coal to be practical.

In 1773, Marquis Claude de Jouffroy d'Ab-bans built a **steamship** in France utilizing a steam engine imported from England that had been built by James E. Watt. Although the design was basically sound, Watts' engine proved to be too heavy for the boat, which sank shortly after it was launched into the Seine River in Paris.

In 1787, two Americans, John Fitch and James Rumsey, constructed a steam-powered rowboat, which had a steam engine that drove two poles connected to rows of oars. The prototype succeeded in its first test, which was witnessed both by George Washington and Benjamin Franklin, and the two inventors were issued a government license to develop steam navigation in the United States. However, their subsequent steamboats didn't work as well as the prototype, and Fitch drowned himself after an unsuccessful attempt to resell the concept in France.

Rumsey then collaborated with another American inventor, Robert Fulton, who had been working on submarines in France. With the aid of Robert R. Livingston, the American ambassador to France, the two men built a demonstration steamboat in 1803. Back in the United States in 1807, again with Livingston's help, Fulton built a full-size steamboat named Clermont (after Livingston's Hudson Valley home) to run on the Hudson River. The Clermont was a great success, and soon there were many steamboats plying American rivers.

In 1818, Captain Moses Rogers of Savannah, Georgia, produced what was destined to be the world's first ocean-going steamship. On May 26, 1819, Rogers set out from Savannah for Europe, arriving in Liverpool, England, in twenty-five days.

The invention of **photography** evolved from experiments both with lenses that could project an image onto a surface and light-sensitive materials that could record the projected images. The lens experiments have their roots in a camera obscura, in which sunlight, reflected off an object and directed through a small hole into a darkroom or box, will project an inverted image of the object onto the opposite wall. Used by Leonardo da Vinci, a **camera obscura** was named by Neapolitan Giambattista della Porta in 1558. By the early nineteenth century, lens-making had developed to the point where clear, distinct images could be projected.

A camera obscura

In 1727, a German doctor named J. H. Schulze discovered that silver chloride was darkened by exposure to light. In England, Humphrey Davy conducted further experiments with silver chloride and made prints of leaves and other objects, but he had no way of preserving his images, which quickly turned black all over. Experiments in the quest for chemical processes to aid in capturing photographic images were conducted in both France and England. In 1824, Joseph Nicéphore Nièpce discovered that a sun-printed image could be permanently fixed by coating a metal plate with bitumen before placing it in a camera obscura for a prolonged exposure. The resulting picture was called a **heliotype**.

In 1829, Nièpce entered a partnership with Louis-Jacques Daguerre to perfect this method. In 1839, Daguerre unveiled the daguerreotype process. Based on Nièpce's discovery, it produced fixed photographic images on copper plates. Although the **daguerreotype** is regarded as the first common photographic process, it still used the toxic vapors of heated mercury to process images.

Also in the 1830s, William Henry Fox Talbot in England, who had been experimenting with silver iodide and silver nitrate coated papers, unveiled the **calotype** process, in which negative images were fixed on paper. From these original negatives—as we know them today—many positive contact prints could be made. The next step was to coat transparent glass plates with a photosensitive emulsion, a method which provided negatives from which prints of unprecedented clarity could be made.

The greatest drawback to using these photographic plates was that they had to be coated with emulsion and exposed while wet. In 1878, George Eastman of Rochester, New York, introduced an advanced **dry plate** process whereby plates could be prepared ahead of time and exposed while dry. A year later, he invented an emulsion coating machine that allowed him to manufacture plates in quantity.

In 1889, Eastman began marketing strips of celluloid with emulsion on them that could be used to make a series of photographic negatives. This idea of a "roll of film" cranked through a camera quickly and became the basis of nearly all popular photography, paving the way for motion pictures, too. The enterprise that Eastman founded, the **Eastman Kodak Company**, became the leading manufacturer of photographic products in the world.

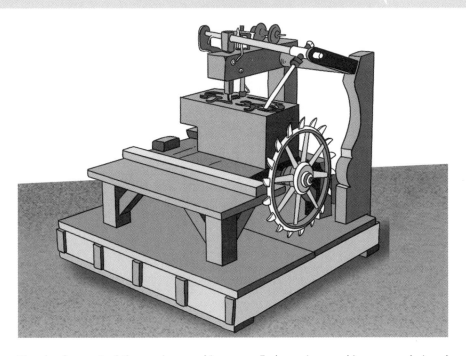

The development of the **sewing machine** made possible the mass production of clothing on a much larger scale than had ever been possible with hand-stitching. The first step was patented in 1755 by American inventor Charles T. Wiesenthal, who designed a double-pointed needle to eliminate the need for turning the needle around with each stitch.

In 1830, Barthélemy Thimonnier of Saint-Étienne, France, used the **double-pointed needle** as the basis for the first sewing machine put to practical use. He attached the needle to a wheel-driven connecting rod that drove the needle up and down. In 1834, American Walter Hunt designed a **double-thread shuttle machine**. In 1846, Elias Howe patented the **lock-stitch sewing machine**, and in 1849, Benjamin Wilson introduced an automatic feeding system. In 1849, Hunt also patented, but failed to profit from, the **safety pin**.

Early sewing machines were designed for industrial application, but in 1851, Isaac Merritt Singer, a machinist from Boston, Massachusetts, introduced the first sewing machine scaled for home use. Although Singer's early machines were based on Howe's concept, he patented the rigid arm for holding the needle and a vertical bar to hold the cloth down against the upward stroke of the needle. Singer also developed the **continuous stitch machine** and went on to found the Singer Sewing Machine Company, which became one of the world's largest manufacturers of personal sewing machines.

Although the introduction of powered machinery revolutionized agriculture and increased food production, the story of the mechanization of harvesting is a curious one. Roman historian Pliny the Younger described a harvesting machine that was in use by Celtic people in Gaul in 100 CE, but this machine was never adapted for use elsewhere and seems to have fallen out of use after 500 CE.

The technology was not reinvented until the first decade of the nineteenth century, when mechanized reaping machines appeared in England. In 1826, Patrick Bell built a **plane reaper** that cut and gathered wheat with serrated rotary blades. In the United States, Robert McCormick attempted to build an automatic, horse-drawn reaper that could be mass-produced. He abandoned this project, but inspired his son Cyrus, who invented the practical **mechanical harvester** in 1831 and patented it in 1834.

Cyrus McCormick's reaper was an immediate success, and the McCormick Harvesting Machine Company in Chicago produced thousands of machines. In 1902, the company merged with Deering Harvester Company to form the International Harvester Company. The self-propelled **combine harvester**, common throughout the world today, was developed in 1888, but it was not mass-produced until 1944, when it was used in the United States to harvest immense quantities of grain necessary to sustain a nation at war.

Anesthesia is derived from the Greek word *anaesthetos, meaning "want of feeling."* It was developed as a means of making a medical patient unconscious via **general anesthesia** or numbing a portion of the patient's body with **local anesthesia** in order to perform surgery with the patient not reacting to pain. The first use of a chemical general anesthetic was in 1834 by Sir James Young Simpson of Edinburgh, Scotland, who used **chloroform** in obstetrics. After Queen Victoria was chloroformed during the delivery of her seventh child, the chemical came into widespread use.

On December 10, 1844, Gardner Quincy Colton displayed the wonders of **nitrous oxide**, or "**laughing gas**," at Union Hall in Hartford, Connecticut. As his show progressed, a man who had inhaled the gas rushed through the hall pursued by another "volunteer." The pursuer tripped, fell to the floor, and hurt his leg, but felt no pain.

General anesthesia was first used in surgery in the United States when Dr. Crawford Williamson Long used **ether** on his patients in 1842. In September 1846, at the suggestion of the chemist Dr. Charles Thomas Jackson, Dr. William Thomas Green Morton, a dentist, decided to replace nitrous oxide with ether. On September 30, 1846, he put Eben H. Frost under ether, then freed him painlessly of an abscessed tooth. Ether was next used by Dr. Morton and Dr. John Collins Warren at Massachusetts General Hospital in a neck tumor operation on October 14, 1846. Thereafter, ether, like chloroform, came into general use.

The first local anesthesia was **cocaine**, which was used after 1884. In 1904, it was replaced with **novocaine**, which is procaine hydrochloride. The first synthesized intravenous anesthesia, a barbital originally marketed under the trade name **Veronal**, was administered in 1902. It was superseded by other **barbiturates** such as **Amytal, Nembutal** (pentobarbital sodium), and **Pentothal** (theopental sodium) after 1930.

The concept of a gun that did not require a time-consuming reloading process before every shot had been a dream of military strategists and designers since the fifteenth century. It was the precision and mass production capability introduced during the Industrial Revolution that finally made this dream attainable.

The first **repeating pistol**, the **revolver**, was originated by Samuel Colt of Paterson, New Jersey, based on a suggestion made by Samuel H. Walker, a Texas Ranger. Colt's revolver fired six shots stored in a cylinder that rotated them into firing position one at a time.

While working at the Volcanic Arms Company in New Haven, Connecticut, Benjamin Tyler Henry designed the first **repeating rifle**. Shortly after Henry joined the company in 1857, it went bankrupt and was taken over by Oliver F. Winchester. The Henry rifle, as his invention was known, was offered to the U.S. Army, which initially rejected the idea. However, when the Civil War began, the Connecticut militia, armed with the new weapon, proved its worth in the heat of battle.

In 1866, Volcanic Arms changed its name to the Winchester Repeating Arms Company and soon was manufacturing thousands of lever action rifles. The **Winchester Model 1873**, introduced in 1873, used the world's first **centerfire cartridge** and was destined to become the standard repeating rifle for many generations to come. It remained in production from 1873 until 1924, with over seventy-two thousand units being manufactured during that time. Many Model 1873s are still in use today, and its familiar profile lives on in the **Model 94**, also manufactured by Winchester.

A Volcanic rifle

The **electric motor** is based on the principle that like poles of a magnet repel one another. In a simple form of an electric motor, a wire-wound armature, in which a magnetic field can be induced by an electric current, is mounted on a rotating shaft and balanced next to a magnet called the "field" magnet. As one pole of the magnet repels the similarly induced pole of the armature, the opposite pole on the similar side of the armature will likewise be repelled by the similar pole of the magnet. This repulsion will produce a torque, and the armature will start revolving. The repulsion between like poles is supplemented by the attraction between unlike poles, and the armature will continue revolving to bring its north pole in line with the south pole and its south pole with the north pole of the field magnet. Just as this conjunction is reached, the action of the commutator—a rotating contractor on the armature shaft—reverses the current in the armature windings. What had been the north pole of the armature suddenly becomes the south pole, and vice versa. Momentum carries the armature past this dead center, and the reversed forces of attraction and repulsion send it on around to its former position, where the commutator again reverses the current. This repeats indefinitely.

In 1838, Moritz Hermann von Jacobi, a German physicist working in Russia, made what may be the first electric motor, which he used to power a small paddleboat. In 1844, Paul Gustave Froment began building small, direct current electric motors in France to power circulating machines. His colleague Hippolyte Fontaine built the first large-scale electric motor in 1873, and by 1885, such motors were being used to power street cars.

In 1878, Fontaine, working with the Belgian Zénobe Gramme, invented the **alternator**, a device for turning **direct current (DC)** into **alternating current (AC)**, which is more easily transmuted than DC. Ernst Werner von Siemens began manufacturing alternators in his native Germany that same year. In 1885, Italian physicist Galileo Ferraris discovered the rotating magnetic field and invented the **alternating current synchronous motor**, which has a variable speed capability.

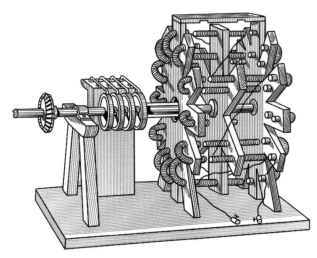

Moritz Herman von Jacobi's electric motor

Telegraphy is defined as the process of sending a coded message over a long distance by means of electricity. The **telegraph** is the machine that makes this possible. The term telegraph is derived from a combination of the Greek roots *tele* meaning "far" and *graph* meaning "writing."

The sending of coded messages dates back to ancient times. In ancient Greece, Clytemnestra learned of Troy's defeat by Agamemnon in 1084 BCE by means of a series of fires built on a distant hillside. Native Americans used a system of transmitting messages with puffs of smoke visible for miles, and ships at sea still use signal flags and flashes of light to communicate.

In 1791, Abbe Claude Chappe coined the term **optical telegraph** to describe his use of a series of towers to relay a message that was visible by one tower from the one before it. Chappe's system involved a string of 120 towers that could convey a message between Paris and the Mediterranean in less than an hour, which was far less time than the fastest horse and rider.

All of these systems depended on visible signals. Telegraphy was a major breakthrough in communications because it made instant communication possible between two people who were out of sight from one another. The idea of sending coded messages by means of electricity dates back to the early eighteenth century. Georges Louis Lesage in Switzerland in 1774 developed a machine that transmitted signals by means of separate wires dedicated to each letter of the alphabet. His system was based on the writings of a mysterious Scottish inventor known only as "C.M.," who had published a similar scheme in 1753.

After Lesage, there were many efforts to refine the telegraph. These were carried out by Chappe in France, Carl Friedrich Gauss and Wilhelm Eduard Weber in Germany, and Alessandro Volta in Italy. Based on the tests carried out by these men, several experimental telegraph lines were set up.

However, the first practical telegraph system was developed by the American inventor Samuel F. B. Morse. Morse, in collaboration with fellow inventor Alfred Vail, also devised the **Morse Code**, which consisted of a series of taps of a key that made electrical contact. Each letter of Morse's alphabet consisted of short taps (dots) combined with longer contacts (dashes), and this system became the universal "language" of the telegraph.

Morse first demonstrated his telegraph to President Martin Van Buren on February 21, 1838, and by 1843, a workable commercial telegraph line was in place between Washington and Baltimore. Within the next two years, most major American and European cities were connected by telegraph, and in the 1850s, England and Sweden were linked to continental Europe by means of underwater cables. Europe and America were joined by an underwater cable between Newfoundland and Ireland in 1858, which was opened with a ninety-word message from Queen Victoria to President James Buchanan.

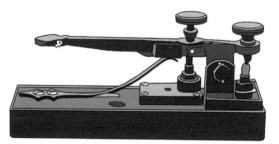

The idea behind the device known in the United States as the **elevator**, in Britain as the **lift,** and in France as the *ascenseur* dates back to first-century Rome. Vitruvius described in first century BCE the use of a counterweight and pulley system to move people up and down in multistory buildings. Louis XV had a "fly chair" system installed at Versailles, and other similar early mechanisms have been described elsewhere. However, it was the American inventor Elisha Graves Otis who patented the first practical and safe elevator in 1851. The Otis Safety Elevator used a system of ratchets or claws to stop the passenger cage from falling if the cable that raised and lowered it were to break.

The Otis Safety Elevator was demonstrated at the Crystal Palace Expo in New York City in 1854. Six years later, Otis improved his own design by introducing an independent reversible steam engine that was directly connected to the lifting mechanism. Within the space of a few years, the Otis invention had revolutionized architecture by making it possible to build office and apartment buildings that were taller than three or four stories. In 1871, the hydraulic elevator was introduced, and in 1889, the first commercial electrically powered elevator was installed.

The most common of all over-the-counter pain relievers has been available in its present form since 1853, but the active ingredient has been known to humans for at least two thousand years. This ingredient, called **acetylsalicylic acid**, is present in the bark of the willow tree and the silver birch tree, as well as in the leaves of such plants as wintergreen and meadowsweet.

Although ancient herbalists knew and prescribed the use of these natural materials for the relief of minor pain, the knowledge was gradually lost as civilization evolved. In 1763, an English doctor named Edward Stone began to study the properties of these plant substances and once again they were prescribed as medicines. In 1853, Carl Frederic Gerhardt in France synthesized acetylsalicylic acid artificially for the first time using a combination of sodium salicylate and acetyl chloride. Gerhardt's breakthrough permitted the widespread manufacture of acetylsalicylic acid.

The name **"aspirin"** was originally a brand name used by the Bayer Company in Germany, but as use of the product spread rapidly, the name became so common that was accepted as a generic term. Today, aspirin is the common name of acetylsalicylic acid in the form of an over-the-counter pain reliever.

An advertisement for aspirin from the 1910s

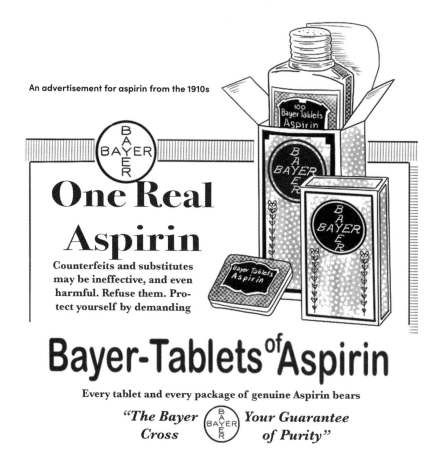

Even though humans have known for centuries that keeping food cold will preserve it, the only way they had to keep it that way was to pack it in natural ice or snow. At some point, perhaps in fourteenth-century China or seventeenth-century Italy, it was discovered that the evaporation of brine (salt water) absorbed heat and therefore a container placed in brine would stay cold.

During the nineteenth century, numerous experimental devices were developed to achieve practical artificial refrigeration. **Compressed ether machines** were built in Pennsylvania by Oliver Evans in 1805 and in Australia by James Harrison in 1855, and Dr. John Gorrie in Florida built an **expanding-air cooling machine** in 1844.

The first significant step toward success in the quest for a practical refrigeration system was made in 1859 by Ferdinand Carré in France, who devised a system whereby a refrigerant—a volatile liquid such as ammonia—was circulated by a compressor around the container to be kept cold. In 1874, Raoul Pictet of Switzerland designed a similar compressor system using sulfur dioxide instead of ammonia as the refrigerant. His machine was later used to create the world's first artificial skating rink in London.

Although Carré's machine was the first to find a practical commercial application, it proved to be cumbersome and immobile. Specifically, it didn't meet the needs of shippers who wished to transport perishables. The first practical and portable **compressor refrigeration machine** was built in Munich in 1874 by Karl von Linde. In his early models, he used methyl ether, which is very explosive, but changed to an ammonia cycle in 1876. Meanwhile, Carré continued to refine his invention, and in 1877, he designed a system for the *Paraguay*, the world's first refrigerated ship that would transport frozen meat from Argentina to France.

At this time, restaurants and homes had "ice boxes," which had an insulated compartment for ice and another for food. The ice was replaced periodically with new blocks purchased from the "iceman," whose wagon was a common sight on the streets.

The first **refrigerator**, as opposed to the simple ice box, designed for home use was the Domelre, which was manufactured in Chicago in 1913. A number of other competing machines quickly appeared, but in 1918, Kelvinator marketed a much more practical home refrigerator. Frigidaire followed with their model in 1919, and General Electric offered the first **hermetically sealed refrigerator compressor** in 1926. The familiar dual temperature refrigerator in use today, with one section for frozen food and a second for chilled food, was introduced into mass production by General Electric in 1939.

Rapid, continuous rate of fire has always been important in warfare. From bows and arrows to guns, designers sought a way to reduce the amount of time required to reload the weapon after a shot had been fired. The first step toward increasing the rate of fire was Samuel Colt's **revolver** in 1836 and Benjamin Tyler Henry's **repeating rifle** in 1860 (see no. 42). In each case, a second shot could be fired within seconds of the first, but the shots were not continuous.

Numerous attempts to develop a continuously firing gun were undertaken in the early nineteenth century, but the first practical weapon was the **Gatling gun**, invented by Richard Jordan Gatling in 1862. This gun was actually a cluster of six guns fed by a cylindrical drum loader located above the weapon, which was powered by a hand crank. The gun entered limited service with the Union Army during the American Civil War and proved extremely deadly. A similar weapon, the French **Montigny mitrailleuse**, was used in the Franco-Prussian War in 1870.

The Gatling gun was capable of four hundred shots per minute, but this was dependent on how quickly the operator turned the crank. The first fully automatic, continuous machine gun was invented in the United States by Hiram Maxim in 1884. By using the recoil energy of one shot to eject the cartridge and bring a second round into the firing chamber, the Maxim machine gun could fire a continuous six hundred rounds per minute. In 1892, another American, John Moses Browning, developed an improved **machine gun** that used the gases produced during firing to power the gun, and this design was copied in France into the design of the **Hotchkiss machine gun**.

This same principle has been used for most machine guns designed in the twentieth century, although Gatling's idea was revived in the 1960s during the development of the **Vulcan automatic cannon**, a multiple-barrel aircraft armament capable of firing 7,200 rounds per minute.

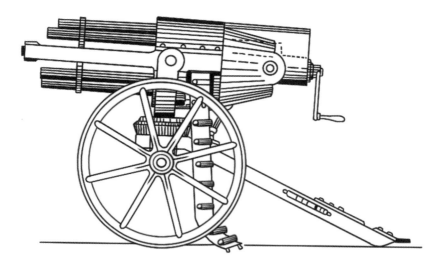

From the eleventh to the nineteenth century, gunpowder was humankind's only workable explosive. In 1846, the Italian chemist Ascanio Sobrero created a new, vastly more lethal explosive chemical that he named **nitroglycerin**. Made of two parts sulfuric acid and one part nitric acid, nitroglycerin was highly unstable. Because of this, it was considered very perilous to handle. At the same time, it tended not to detonate at all if used in extremely cold weather.

After his father was killed in an explosion at the family's nitroglycerin factory in 1862, Swedish chemist Alfred Nobel began a series of experiments to find a more stable nitroglycerin-based explosive that could serve as a replacement for gunpowder when an explosive was called for in civil engineering projects such as tunnel and road building. The result was a product consisting of sticks of charcoal or **kieselguhr** (a.k.a. **porous silica**), which he treated with nitroglycerin. Nobel called this **dynamite**. His invention proved to be more stable than pure nitroglycerin and three to four times more powerful than gunpowder. After first inventing it in 1866, Nobel continued to improve dynamite to make it less hazardous and more reliable in cold weather.

In 1876, Nobel invented **gelatinous dynamite** and other explosive gelignites that eventually evolved into today's plastic explosives. In 1887, he developed a nitroglycerin/nitrocellulose product for propelling artillery shells, which he called **ballistite**, but which was manufactured in England as **cordite**.

The problem of the effectiveness of dynamite in freezing temperatures was finally solved in 1907 by Nobel's firm by blending the nitroglycerin with **TNT (trinitrotoluene)**, a substance invented in Sweden in 1863 by J. Wilbrand. TNT became so universally accepted that its explosive qualities became the benchmark by which all explosives—even nuclear explosives—are measured. In fact, when people speak of the megatonnage of a nuclear bomb, megatons of TNT is the unit of measurement that is used.

Alfred Nobel is also known today as the originator of the **Nobel Prize**, which, with the exception of 1940–1942, has been awarded annually since 1901 to leading figures in the fields of physics, chemistry, physiology or medicine, and literature. There is also an annual Nobel Peace Prize bestowed on a person or an organization that has done the most to promote world peace.

Nitroglycerin and sticks of dynamite

The idea behind the **typewriter** was to apply the concept of movable type developed by Johannes Gutenberg in the invention of the printing press in the fifteenth century to a machine for individual use. Descriptions of such mechanical writing machines date to the early eighteenth century. In 1714, a patent for something like a typewriter was granted to a man named Henry Mill in England, but no example of Mill's invention survives.

In 1829, William Burt from Detroit, Michigan, patented his **typographer** that had characters arranged on a rotating frame. However, Burt's machine, and many of those that followed, were cumbersome, hard to use, unreliable, and often slower in producing a letter than writing it by hand.

Finally, in June 1868, a Milwaukee, Wisconsin-based printer named Christopher Latham Sholes patented the first useful typewriter after completing it the previous year. He licensed his patent to Remington & Sons of Ilion, New York, a noted American gunmaker. In 1874, the Remington Model 1, the first commercial typewriter, was placed on the market. Remington remained a leading manufacturer of typewriters well into the twentieth century.

Based on Sholes' mechanical typewriter, the first **electric typewriter** was built by Thomas Alva Edison in the United States in 1872, but the widespread use of electric typewriters was not common until the 1950s.

The **electronic typewriter**—a typewriter with an electronic "memory" capable of storing text—first appeared in 1978. It was developed independently by the Olivetti Company in Italy and the Casio Company in Japan. This was an important predecessor to electronic word processors that would be developed in the coming decades.

The idea of the **vacuum cleaner**—basically an air pump used in reverse—was the brainchild of American inventor Ives McGaffey. His prototype machine, which he designed in 1868, was called an **aspirator**. Powered by a steam engine, the aspirator was a huge, noisy device suitable only for large, industrial applications. In 1901, Hubert Cecil Booth in England, the owner of the Vacuum Cleaning Company, was the first to build an aspirator powered by an electric motor, but it was also bulky in size and unwieldy to use.

In 1907, American James Murray Spangler constructed a light, conveniently operated electric vacuum cleaning machine. He sold his invention to a harness maker named William H. Hoover, who began manufacturing the machines as the Hoover Model 0. Today, Hoover is still one of the leading makers of vacuum cleaners in the world. Vacuum cleaners were considered a luxury item for several decades, but after World War II, they became more and more common in middle-class households.

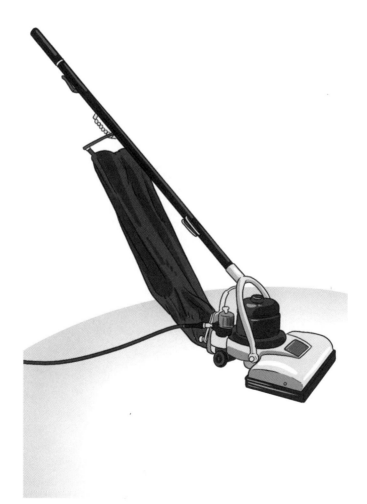

Plastic, in its many diverse forms, is a family of synthetic materials that can duplicate and improve on the properties of many natural materials. Plastic can be formulated to function in many ways that wood usually does, and it is virtually impervious to decay. In many cases, it can be used as a substitute for metal, but it is lighter and not subject to corrosion.

The forerunner of modern plastics is celluloid, which was invented in the 1860s and 1870s by printer John Wesley Hyatt, who developed celluloid in response to a $10,000 prize offered for the invention of a replacement for ivory in the manufacture of billiard balls. Hyatt created celluloid by mixing cellulose nitrate, which is derived from wood or cotton, with camphor at high temperatures. In the late nineteenth century, celluloid was used for a variety of things such as small containers, utensil handles, and piano keys.

The next step in the evolution of plastics was Bakelite, a synthetic thermosetting resin developed in the United States in 1907 by Belgian-born chemist Leo Hendrik Baekeland. Bakelite was a very versatile, moldable material which was used during the first half of the twentieth century for such things as electrical insulators, telephones, and other common objects. Although Bakelite was a revolutionary invention, its major drawback was its brittleness.

Two other important modern plastics were the flexible polyvinyl chloride, known commonly as PVC, and the more rigid polystyrene. Both were developed in Germany in 1913 and 1929, respectively, but did not come into widespread use until after World War II.

Polyethylene, which today is used for everything from light, inexpensive dishware to packaging and laundry bags, was developed in 1933 by Imperial Chemical Industries (ICI) in England. Polyethylene was created by subjecting an ethylene polymer to high pressure. It was improved in 1954 by Karl Ziegler in Germany, who, along with Giulio Natta of Italy, won the 1963 Nobel Prize for his work. Since that time, polyethylene has joined vinyl and styrene and their variants as the most used plastics in the world (see no. 57 and no. 75).

Chemists can combine many different materials to create many different kinds of plastics

Probably no means of communication has revolutionized the daily lives of ordinary people more than the **telephone**. Simply described, it is a system that converts sound—specifically the human voice—to electrical impulses of various frequencies and then back to a tone that sounds like the original voice. In 1831, English scientist Michael Faraday proved that vibrations of metal could be converted to electrical impulses. This was the technological basis of the telephone, but no one actually used this system to transmit sound until 1861. In that year, Johann Philip Reis in Germany is said to have built a simple apparatus that changed sound to electricity and back again to sound. A crude device, it was incapable of transmitting most frequencies, and it was never fully developed.

A practical telephone was invented independently by two men working in the United States: Elisha Gray and Scottish-born Alexander Graham Bell. Incredibly, both men filed for a patent on their designs at the New York patent office on February 14, 1876, with Bell beating Gray by only two hours!

Although Gray had built the first steel diaphragm/electromagnet receiver in 1874, he was not able to master the design of a workable transmitter until after Bell had. Bell had worked tirelessly, experimenting with various types of mechanisms, while Gray had become discouraged.

According to the famous story, the first fully intelligible telephone call occurred on March 6, 1876, when Bell, in one room, called to his assistant in another room: "Come here, Watson," Bell directed. "I want you."

Watson heard the request through a receiver connected to the transmitter that Bell had designed, and what followed is a history of the founding of the Bell Telephone Company (later AT&T), which grew to be the largest telephone company in the world.

The first telephone system, known as an **exchange**, or a practical means of communicating between many people with telephones, was installed in Hartford, Connecticut, in 1877, and the first exchange linking two major cities was established between New York and Boston in 1883. The first exchange outside the United States was built in London in 1879. The exchange involved a group of **operators** working at a large **switchboard**. The operators would answer an incoming telephone call and connect it manually to the party being called. The first **automatic telephone exchange** was patented by Almon Strowger of Kansas City in 1889 and installed in 1892, but manual switchboards remained in common use until the middle of the twentieth century.

The coin-operated **pay telephone** was patented by William Gray of Hartford, Connecticut, in 1889. The first **rotary dial** telephone was developed in 1923 by Antoine Barnay in France. The **mobile telephone** was invented by Bell Telephone Company and introduced into New York City police cars in 1924. Although the first commercial mobile telephone service became available in St. Louis, Missouri, in 1946, the mobile telephone would not become common for another four decades.

In 1978, American Telephone and Telegraph's (AT&T) Bell Laboratories began testing a mobile telephone system based on hexagonal geographical regions called **cells**. As the caller's vehicle passed from one cell to another, an automatic switching system would transfer the telephone call to another cell without interruption. The **cellular telephone** system entered nationwide usage in the United States in 1981.

◆ James E. Watt's steam engine, invented in the eighteenth century, powered the Industrial Revolution of the nineteenth century. It was the invention of the **practical internal-combustion engine** that made possible the Industrial Revolution of the twentieth century, with its airplanes, automobiles, and other engine-driven machines.

Just as with the steam engine, there were many internal-combustion engines built before a practical model was invented. These machines have a mixture of combustible fuel, such as gasoline, and air that is forced into a cylinder where they are compressed and then ignited by a spark. The resulting combustion causes pressure within the cylinder, driving a piston away from the spark and turning a crankshaft.

There were numerous attempts to build a workable internal-combustion engine in the early nineteenth century, but the first successful model was constructed in 1860 by the Belgian-born French inventor Étienne Lenoir. Lenoir's invention, a **two-stroke engine**, did not make use of a compression of fuel before ignition. This step was added by American George Brayton in 1873. In the meantime, Germans Nikolaus August Otto and Eugen Langen invented an **"air-breathing" engine** in 1876 that greatly improved the fuel efficiency of internal-combustion engines.

However, the greatest breakthrough in terms of efficiency and power, was the invention of the **four-stroke engine**, in which every fourth stroke of the piston was a power, or working, stroke. The four-stroke process had been designed in 1862 by French engineer Alphonse Eugene Beau de Rochas, but he never built a practical working model. It was Nikolaus Otto who succeeded in building and patenting the first four-stroke internal-combustion engine in 1876. Thus, although the theory might have originated with de Rochas, Otto was the one able to produce the first successful model.

The four-cycle internal-combustion engine operates on the principle of four strokes of the piston within the cylinder, with the piston plunging into the cylinder on the even numbered strokes: (1) **induction**, as the fuel is pulled into the cylinder; (2) **compression**, as the fuel is compressed by an upward stroke of the piston, (3) **combustion**, as the spark ignites the fuel; and (4) **exhaust**, as the burned gases are pushed out.

As it continued to evolve, the four-stroke engine proved to be more powerful than the two-stroke engine. Although Dugald Clark in England produced a much-improved two-stroke engine in 1879, four-stroke engines capable of over 100 hp were soon being built. Ultimately, the four-stroke internal-combustion engine successfully challenged the steam engine as the machine that would provide the power that would revolutionize transportation in the twentieth century.

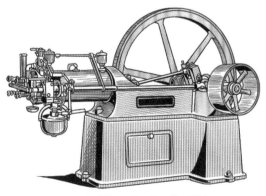

An Otto engine from the 1880s

Like so many things we take for granted today, the idea of recording sound seemed like fiction in the nineteenth century. Two parallel, independent experimental projects, undertaken by Charles Cros in France and Thomas Alva Edison in the United States, led to the invention of the **phonograph** in 1877. The Cros device, unveiled in April, involved a glass cylinder coated with lamp black (soot) into which grooves had been etched by a stylus set to vibrate with sound waves. These grooves were then photoengraved onto a steel cylinder.

In August, Edison displayed a cylinder wrapped in a thin sheet of foil and etched with a needle. There is no known evidence that the Cros phonograph actually worked, but on December 6, 1877, Edison made a recording of himself reciting "Mary Had a Little Lamb" that still survives today. The first Edison phonograph, which he called a **talking machine**, was powered by a hand crank, but the sound tempo was so inconsistent that he designed one with an electric motor in 1878.

An improved phonograph model was developed in 1886 by Edison in partnership with Charles Sumner Tainter and Chichester Bell, a cousin of Alexander Graham Bell. While the Edison machine recorded sound on cylinders, German-born American Emil Berliner invented a machine in 1887 that he called the **gramophone**, which used flat discs. This system became the standard, and by the turn of the century, thousands had been sold in the United States and in Europe. In 1888, Berliner returned to Germany to form the Deutsche Gramophone Gesellschaft (DGG), which is still the world's most important classical recording music company today.

Early discs, known as **records**, were first made of wax-coated zinc that evolved to shellac and then to plastic and eventually to vinyl. The first records rotated at 78 revolutions per minute (rpm), but they were later replaced by the 33-rpm, long-playing (LP) record, which was introduced in the United States in 1948 by Columbia Broadcasting System (CBS). Early records were **monaural**, i.e., they'd had only one soundtrack. **Stereophonic** (two-track sound) was introduced in England by EMI in 1933, but it was not until the late 1960s that most records sold were stereo. The record itself was largely replaced in the 1980s by the **compact disc** (see no. 65 and no. 95).

The **electric light**, one of the everyday conveniences that most affects our lives, was invented in 1879 simultaneously by Thomas Alva Edison in the United States and Sir Joseph Wilson Swan in England.

However, the story of the electric light actually goes back to 1811, when Sir Humphrey Davy discovered that an electrical arc passed between two poles and produced light. In 1841, experimental arc lights were installed as public lighting along the Place de la Concorde in Paris. Other experiments were undertaken in Europe and America, but the **arc light** eventually proved impractical because it burned out too quickly. Inventors continued to grapple with the problem of developing a reliable electric light that would be practical for both home and public use as a viable alternative to gas light.

The solution lay not in an electrical arc in open space, but in electricity passed through a **filament**. The breakthrough theory became known as the **Joule effect** after James Prescott Joule, who theorized that electrical current, if passed through a resistant conductor, would glow white-hot with heat energy turning into luminous energy. The problem was devising the right conductor, or filament, and inserting it in a container—or bulb—without oxygen because the presence of oxygen would cause the filament to burn.

Swan was the first to construct an electric light bulb, but he had trouble maintaining a vacuum inside it. Edison solved this problem, and on October 21, 1879, he illuminated a **carbon filament light bulb** that glowed continuously for forty hours. By the end of 1880, he had produced a 16-watt bulb that could last for 1,500 hours, and he began to market his new invention. Thomas Edison eventually proved himself to be one of the most prolific inventors of practical electrical devices in history.

In 1910, William David Coolidge of the General Electric Company of Schenectady, New York, invented the tungsten filament, which further improved the longevity of the light bulb.

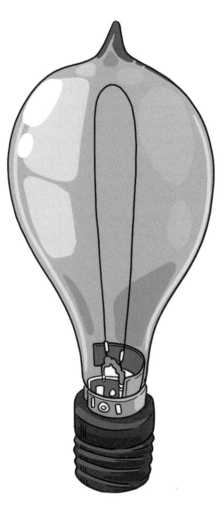

Synthetic fabrics, commonplace today, are desirable because they are not as prone to shrinkage and decomposition as natural fabrics. They are also less expensive than certain natural fibers, such as silk. Indeed, the first semi-synthetic fiber, **rayon**, was designed to emulate the feel and appearance of silk.

Rayon was developed by Louis-Marie-Hilaire Bernigaud, comte de Chardonnet in response to a silkworm disease that was threatening the French silk industry. Originally, rayon was known as "artificial silk," and the term rayon was coined in 1924, derived from "ray," a reference to the fabric's luminescence. Rayon was first made of nitrocellulose from wood pulp, but in 1892, English chemists Charles Cross and Edward Bevan altered the process, converting the **nitrocellulose** to a viscose solution. In 1894, Cross and Bevan patented a process that led to **acetate rayon**. All these processes are still used today to manufacture rayon fabrics.

In the twentieth century, numerous coal and petroleum-based synthetic fabrics were introduced. The first, and probably the most important, was PA6-6, or **nylon**, which was invented by Wallace Hume Carothers in the United States in 1931 and

marketed after 1938 by the DuPont Chemical Company. Nylon is used for a wide variety of products, ranging from bristles and rope to stockings, fishing line and carpets.

Other twentieth-century synthetic fabrics include **Rhovyl** (1941), **polyesters** (1941), **Orlon** (1943), **Rilsan** (1950), and **Tencel** (1972), a type of rayon.

In terms of the lives of average people, there is little doubt that the **automobile** is the most revolutionary invention in the history of transportation since the wheel. The basic premise of the automobile is simple: choose a wheeled vehicle from the many types typically pulled by horses or oxen, add a motor and create a self-propelled, personal transportation vehicle.

The earliest ancestor of the modern automobile is probably the **fardier**—a three-wheeled, steam-powered, 2.3-mph vehicle built in 1771 by Nicolas-Joseph Cugnot for the French minister of war. This cumbersome machine was never put into production because it was much slower and harder to operate than a horse-drawn vehicle.

Amédée Bollée, also a French inventor, built an improved twelve-passenger steam car in 1873, but the steam engine proved impractical for a machine that was intended to challenge the speed of a horse-and-buggy. The invention of the practical automobile had to await the invention of a workable internal-combustion engine.

The milestone vehicle was built in Germany in 1889 by Gottlieb Daimler and Wilhelm Maybach. Powered by a 1.5-hp, two-cylinder gasoline engine, it had a four-speed transmission and traveled at 10 miles per hour (16 kilometers per hour).

The gasoline-powered automobile, or motor car, remained largely a curiosity for the rest of the nineteenth century, with only a handful being manufactured in Europe and the United States. The first automobile to be produced in quantity was the 1901 **Curved Dash Oldsmobile**, which was built in the United States by Ransom E. Olds.

Modern automobile mass production, and indeed the invention of the **modern industrial assembly line**, is credited to Henry Ford of Detroit, Michigan, who had built his first gasoline-powered car in 1896. Ford began producing his **Model T** in 1908, and by 1927, when it was discontinued, over 18 million had rolled off the assembly line.

The invention of **motion pictures** was a complex process involving numerous other breakthroughs. The movies as we know them today would not have been possible, of course, without photography or sound recording. However, the key idea behind motion pictures came with the discovery that when a series of closely spaced, sequential still pictures—such as that of a child skipping rope or a horse running—are viewed in rapid succession, the viewer experiences the illusion of movement.

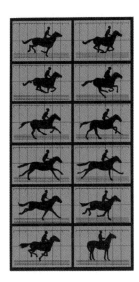

This phenomenon, known as the persistence of vision, was understood by Leonardo da Vinci. In the nineteenth century, inventors produced various handheld devices in which one could view images arranged on a spinning wheel or disk that appeared to move. These included Joseph Plateau's **phenakistoscope** in Belgium (1832), Coleman Sellers' **kinematoscope** in the United States (1861), and Henry Renno Heyl's **phasmatrope** in the United States (1870).

What all these mechanisms had in common was that they used images printed on an opaque surface for direct viewing. The next step in the development leading up to motion pictures occurred in 1889, when William Friese-Greene in England and Thomas Alva Edison in the United States each decided to print multiple images on a transparent material that could be projected. Meanwhile, George Eastman, founder of the Eastman Kodak Company, invented and started to produce **nitrocellulose film** in rolls for use in still cameras (see no. 38).

Edison adapted this for use in his **kinetograph**, which was the first camera specifically designed to film motion pictures, and his **kinetoscope**, which was the first motion picture projector. Both were patented in 1891, and the kinetoscope had its debut in New York as a peepshow device in 1894.

Edison had failed to patent his inventions abroad, so it was possible for two brothers in France named Auguste and Louis Lumière to build what amounted to an improved version of Edison's kinetograph that they called **cinematographie**. Their improvements allowed for the development of the first large, full-scale projection of motion pictures on a theater wall, which took place at the Grand Café in Paris on March 22, 1895. Edison went on to further refine his process, producing his own projector, the **vitascope**, which led to the first projection of a motion picture in a theater in the United States at Bial's Music Hall in New York City on April 23, 1896.

Later that same year, Edison's former associate, William Dickson, joined with Herman Caster, E. B. Koopman and H. N. Marvin to develop the **biograph**. Like the **vitascope**, but with wider film, it made images much sharper when they were projected. Although Edison had built a movie studio in New Jersey in 1893, Dickson's New York-based company, called American Mutoscope Company (later Biograph Company), was the first motion picture production company.

Scottish physicist and chemist Sir James Dewar was a pioneer in the science of **spectroscopy** and liquefaction of gases. In fact, he was the first person to obtain hydrogen in both liquid and solid states, but his work touches our daily lives in a much simpler, unique invention.

In 1892, he faced the challenge of keeping a baby bottle warm for his young son. He solved the problem by inventing the vacuum bottle, a double-walled, glass container with space between the walls evacuated and sealed to prevent heat transfer. The inner walls are silvered to reduce heat loss by radiation. A **vacuum bottle** can maintain its contents for hours at their original temperature, whether hot or cold, but Dewar's mother-in-law, doubting its effectiveness, knitted a woolen cozy for the prototype vacuum bottle, which can still be seen by visiting London's Science Museum.

The vacuum bottles in common use today are virtually identical to Dewar's original creation.

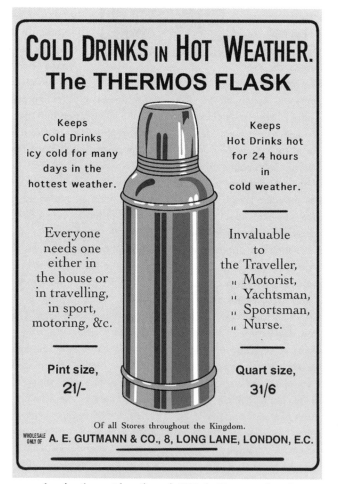

An advertisement from the early 1900s for Thermos, a brand of vacuum bottles

The Sun has always been a source of light and warmth for the Earth and its inhabitants. The use of optically focused sunlight to start fires was theorized by Archimedes and has been used since the development of the first lenses (see no. 24).

In the nineteenth century, Antoine-Laurent Lavoisier in France built the first **solar furnaces**, which were large machines that focused tremendous heat for industrial purposes. In 1878, focused solar energy was used at the Paris World Fair to generate enough heat to drive a small steam engine.

The development of a system to convert the Sun's energy directly into electricity dates from the discovery of the **photovoltaic effect** in 1839 by French physicist Edmond Becquerel. The first **photovoltaic cells** were made in 1888 from selenium covered with a thin gold film by American inventor Charles Fritts. German scientists Julius Elster and Hans Geitel also made selenium cells that converted light to electricity in 1893.

Because early **photoelectric cells** were both expensive and inefficient as they converted only about 1 percent of the incoming light into electricity, they were considered impractical until the dawn of space exploration in the early 1960s. The combination of the discovery of the silicon photoelectric cell by Calvin Fuller and Gordon Pearson at Bell Laboratories in 1954 along with the advent of high-budget, orbiting spacecraft made the **silicon solar cell** a practical device. **Solar cells** were seen as an ideal source of electricity because solar energy is continuous in space, and unlike batteries, solar cells never wear out.

Today, solar cells are standard equipment on all communications, meteorological, and other satellites. Because of their development for spacecraft, silicon-based solar cells are much more advanced than they would have been otherwise and have been adapted for use on Earth. Since the early 1980s, solar cells have been used to power telephones, water heaters, automobiles, and even airplanes.

The idea of a fastening system for flexible materials based on two opposing rows of tiny, interlocking teeth first occurred to American inventor Whitcomb L. Judson in 1890, who perfected and patented the technology in 1893.

The earliest **zippers** or **zip fasteners** were being used in the apparel industry by 1905, but they were not considered practical until an improved version was developed by Gideon Sundback, a Swedish engineer working in the United States. By the 1920s, zippers came into widespread use on clothing, luggage, and many other applications. They have continued to be an essential convenience ever since.

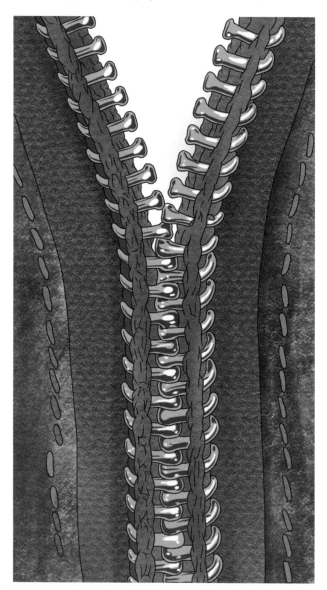

German scientist Heinrich Hertz

Both the invention of the telegraph in 1838 and the telephone in 1875 were enormous leaps forward in communication technology, but the people using them had to be linked by a continuous conductor. If the conductor—usually a wire—was broken or could not be run, then communication was impossible.

In 1887, the German scientist Heinrich Hertz discovered **radio waves**, but it was the Italian physicist Guglielmo Marconi who first adapted them for use in communication. In 1895, Marconi succeeded in transmitting a **wireless electronic message** over 1.5 miles near his home in Bologna, Italy. In 1898, Eugène Ducretet and Ernest Roger made a wireless transmission across the city of Paris, and on March 28, 1899, Marconi sent the first international wireless message from Dover, England, to Wimereux, France—a distance of 31 miles. Two years later, on December 12, 1901, Marconi completed the first intercontinental wireless transmission between Poldhu, England, and a receiving station in Newfoundland, approximately 2,100 miles away.

In 1903, Marconi established a transmission station with the identifying call letters "WCC" in South Wellfleet, Massachusetts. The dedication ceremonies included an exchange of greetings between President Theodore Roosevelt and King Edward VII. In 1904, Marconi entered into an agreement with the Cunard steamship line to create the first **ship-to-shore communications system**. This system proved to be a vital factor in saving lives in the event of maritime disasters, such as the sinking of the RMS *Titanic* in 1912.

Rudolf Diesel developed the revolutionary engine that bears his name as a means of increasing efficiency while lowering the cost of operation.

The **diesel engine** is an internal-combustion engine that differs from a conventional internal-combustion engine in that it uses compression rather than an electric spark to ignite the fuel and air mixture in the cylinder. It works on the principle that compression creates heat (see no. 54).

The idea behind the compression-ignition combustion engine was explored by Nicolas Léonard Sadi Carnot in 1824, but Rudolf Diesel patented the first practical design in 1892, which was later revised in 1893. However, he did not actually build a working compression-ignition combustion engine until 1897. The first commercial application of the diesel engine occurred in the United States a year later.

Various attempts have been made toward building a practical, solid-fuel internal-combustion engine, but none has been successful. In fact, Rudolf Diesel was working on one himself when he mysteriously disappeared from the deck of a ship in 1913 while crossing the English Channel between Harwich, England, and Antwerp, Belgium.

Diesel engines are inherently more efficient than spark-ignited gasoline engines because of their higher compression ratio, which results in a greater expansion ratio pushing the piston in the cylinder. Diesel engines are less costly to operate because they can use fuel that is less refined than gasoline. However, diesel engines are heavier and more complex than gasoline engines. Because of these factors, gasoline engines are used in airplanes, automobiles, and lawnmowers, while diesel engines are usually found in power-generating stations, heavy trucks, locomotives, and ships.

The principle of **magnetic recording** on wire or tape depends on the creation of readable magnetic domains on a very small scale. The theory of magnetic recording was developed by Oberlin Smith in England in 1888, but the first steel wire-based magnetic recorder was built in Denmark by Valdemar Poulsen in 1898. Poulsen called his invention a **telegraphone**.

In 1927, J. A. O'Neill introduced a magnetic recording system in the United States that used ribbons coated with iron oxide. The broader surface of the ribbons allowed a wider spectrum of sound to be recorded simultaneously. In 1928, Fritz Pfleumer in Germany introduced a paper strip system based on the same idea as O'Neill's ribbon, and he sold his idea to German chemical company AEG. They in turn sold it to the BASF company, which replaced the paper with cellulose-acetate strips. In 1934, BASF produced a plastic-backed magnetic recording tape similar to the tape used in cassettes in later decades.

The first commercial tape recording, which featured the London Philharmonic Orchestra, was made by BASF at their Ludwigshafen, Germany, factory on November 19, 1936. At the end of the twentieth century, most home recordings and some commercial recordings were made on **compact audio cassettes**. These were invented by the Dutch electronics firm Koninklijke Philips N.V.—commonly known as Philips—which introduced them to the mass market in 1963. Philips purposely did not patent them, hoping for universal acceptance, which did, in fact, take place.

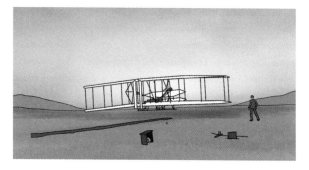

Humankind's dreams of flight date to when our ancestors first regarded birds with envy. Therè were numerous designs for flying machines, including those of Leonardo da Vinci, but none are known to have been practical. The Montgolfier brothers were the first to succeed in sustained human flight using a **balloon** in 1783 (see no. 33). During the nineteenth century, several people, including Jean-Marie Le Bris and Louis-Pierre Mouillard in France and Otto Lilienthal in Germany, built gliders with which they made successful short flights. Still, the idea of a powered and controlled flight in a vehicle heavier than air proved elusive because the only source of mechanized power was the steam engine, which was too heavy to be carried into the air by any early flying machine.

The key to solving this problem was the **internal-combustion engine** (see no. 54). The U.S. government invested a great deal of money in Samuel Pierpont Langley's unsuccessful attempts to build such a machine, and this project was abandoned in December 1903.

At the same time, two men from Ohio, Wilbur Wright and his brother Orville, were also working on an airplane project, which they financed on their own. The Wright brothers shared an interest in aeronautics from youth and built their first unmanned glider in 1896. Between 1900 and 1902 they tested a series of manned gliders.

They recognized that the key to successful powered flight would be the degree of control that the pilot could exercise over his craft. They looked upon their project as an aircraft rather than as a modified kite or as a machine that would be merely steered in the air as a boat was in the water. Their **Wright Flyer** was a fabric-covered biplane with a wooden frame. It was powered by the Wrights' own 12-hp, water-cooled engine driving two propellers by means of chains.

The brothers completed their flyer during the summer of 1903 and took it to North Carolina in December. On December 17, 1903, after several disappointing attempts, Orville took off and flew for twelve seconds, covering 120 feet in the first powered flight of a manned heavier-than-air aircraft in history. By the end of the day, both of the brothers had made two successful flights, with Wilbur covering 852 feet in his last turn at the controls.

They returned to Dayton and went to work on a second flyer, which was essentially the same as the first except for an upgraded 16-hp engine. First flown on May 13, 1904, the **Wright Flyer II** made many successful flights over the next seven months. Like the original flyer, however, it tended to stall in turns, and the Wrights went back to the drawing board. The result was the larger **Wright Flyer III**, which proved to be a much more reliable airplane. In tests near Dayton, it was flown over 34 miles. On October 5, 1905, it set an endurance record of thirty-eight minutes.

Most of today's advanced theories about our place in the greater universe, and in the tiny universe of **atoms** and smaller-than-atoms **sub-atomic particles** that make up all matter, are founded on the work of a shy, German-born physicist named Albert Einstein. Einstein is regarded as being the greatest scientific mind since Isaac Newton. Indeed, his **theory of relativity**, published in its basic form in 1905 and 1915, is so profound that it is still not understood by most people. Einstein demonstrated that time was relative to the speed at which the observer is traveling. He also theorized that the speed at which light travels, which we understand as 186,000 miles per second, is not absolute.

Although Einstein's theory is extremely difficult, he joked about it when he wrote that "by an application of the theory of relativity to the taste of the reader, today in Germany I am called a German man of science; in England I am represented as a Swiss Jew. If I come to be regarded as a bête noire, the description will be reversed and I shall become a Swiss Jew for the Germans, a German for the English."

The essence of Einstein's general theory of relativity is that if matter is converted into energy, the energy released can be shown in the formula $E = mc^2$, where E equals energy, c represents the velocity of light, and m represents mass. The formula implies that a small mass can be converted into a huge amount of energy.

Einstein's discoveries about nuclear energy also explained the nature of stars—including our own Sun—by demonstrating that if the Sun were really on fire, it would have been consumed years ago. In a nuclear reaction, Einstein suggested that huge quantities of light and heat could go on being created, with the loss of only a very small mass. Einstein's theory mathematically explained the theoretical foundation that led to the development of nuclear weapons and reactors in the pursuit of creating nuclear energy.

Radio waves were discovered in 1887 in Germany by Heinrich Hertz, and this paved the way for Guglielmo Marconi's first **wireless communication** in 1895. However, **radio**, as we know it today, involving actual sounds rather than merely the dots and dashes of the Morse Code (see no. 44), was not possible without the invention of the **microphone** and the **Audion tube**. The microphone is a device which converts sounds into electrical impulses, such as in the telephone patented by Bell in 1876. The Audion, an electronic tube, makes it possible to amplify and transmit those complex electrical impulses.

The Audion, invented in 1906 and patented in 1907 by American scientist Lee de Forest, was preceded by the **diode**, invented in 1905 by Marconi's associate Sir John Ambrose Fleming. The diode is a **vacuum tube** containing two **electrodes**, a **cathode,** and an **anode**. The anode is alternately charged positive and negative as it receives radio waves. De Forest advanced the diode design by adding a third electrode, or **control grid**. This addition improved both transmission and reception capabilities.

Up to this time, radio transmitters and receivers were custom-made machines, and the idea of a broadcast intended for a large audience did not become a reality until the advent of the mass-produced **crystal set** radio receiver. It had been discovered that **galena crystals** were particularly sensitive to radio waves, and this led to the development of practical radios for home use about the same time that de Forest introduced his Audion tube.

With all the elements of this new technology available, de Forest sought to demonstrate the potential of radio by arranging for the first ever radio broadcast, featuring the great tenor Enrico Caruso singing Pietro Mascagni's *Cavalleria rusticana* from the Metropolitan Opera House in New York City on January 13, 1910. However, the first regularly scheduled radio programming did not begin until the Westinghouse Company broadcast the November 2, 1920, presidential election results from Pittsburgh, Pennsylvania. In 1922, the British Broadcasting Corporation (BBC) was formed, and it broadcast its first news program on November 14.

Italian physicist Guglielmo Marconi and his radio

The process of instantly transmitting moving images over great distances by means of electromagnetic waves was discussed as a theory in the nineteenth century. Some devices for sending still pictures were actually built. The construction of a device for converting continuously moving images to electricity depended on the discovery of the properties of **selenium**, a chemical element discovered in 1817. Just as the silver compounds

used in photography are sensitive to light, so too is the resistance of selenium to electricity sensitive to light. A parallel development occurred in 1884 when Paul Nipkow in Germany advanced a means for optically converting images into parallel lines of various intensities. Initially, television was the process of recording and transmitting such images by means of selenium cells.

The **iconoscope**, invented in 1924 by Russian American Vladimir Kosma Zworykin, was also important in the development of modern television. With the iconoscope, an image is projected onto a screen of photoelectric cells at the bottom of a cathode tube. Light striking these cells induces a current, whose level of intensity corresponds to the brightness of the cell that releases a video signal during scanning. As such, the iconoscope is the direct ancestor of the **picture tube** used in modern television sets.

Although there were numerous experiments with devices based on Nipkow's discovery, it was Scottish engineer John Logie Baird who built the first practical television (TV). In 1923, he patented an eight-scan-line television system, and in

1926, he demonstrated his **Noctovisor**, which was used for the first public television broadcast in the United Kingdom. In 1927, the Bell Telephone Company broadcast television images from Washington to New York via telephone lines—the first use of television in the United States. In 1928, Baird conducted the first transatlantic television broadcast from London to New York using shortwaves. The BBC began broadcasting regular television programming in 1930 when Baird's improved Noctovisor went on the market. Although Baird's invention was not an immediate commercial success, by 1939, there were twenty thousand television viewers in the United Kingdom. A French television transmitter was installed atop the Eiffel Tower in 1935, and RCA installed one atop New York's Empire State Building in 1936. Because of World War II, television did not become a common fixture in private homes until the late 1940s and early 1950s.

John Baird built the first **color television** system in 1928, and Bell Laboratories devised a parallel system in the United States in 1929. While color television had always been theoretically possible, it did not improve to the point of becoming a commercial practicality until the late 1960s. Early color television sets had three separate tubes for red, blue, and green, but in 1968, Japan's Sony Corporation developed the **Trinitron** tube, in which all three colors were combined into a single tube and a grid permitted a greater color range to reach the viewing screen.

The use of **telefacsimile** machines (**telefax** or **fax**) to transmit images via telephone lines did not become common in American businesses until the late 1980s, but the technology dates back to the nineteenth century. In 1843 in England, Alexander Bain devised an apparatus comprised of two pens connected to two pendulums joined together by a wire. This apparatus could reproduce writing on an electrically conductive surface. In 1862, Italian physicist Giovanni Caselli built a machine he called a **pantelegraph**—possibly a portmanteau of "pantagraph" and "telegraph"—which was based on Bain's invention but also included a synchronizing apparatus. His pantelegraph was used by the French Post & Telegraph agency between Paris and Marseille from 1856 to 1870.

In 1902, Arthur Korn in Germany invented **telephotography**, known in German as *Bildtelegraph*, a means for manually breaking down and transmitting still photographs by means of electrical wires. In 1907, Korn sent the first intercity fax when he transmitted a photograph from Munich to Berlin. In 1925, Édouard Belin in France constructed the **Belinograph**. His invention involved placing an image on a cylinder and scanning it with a powerful light beam that had a photoelectric cell that could convert light or the absence of light into transmittable electrical impulses. The Belinograph process used the basic principle upon which all subsequent facsimile transmission machines would be based. In 1934, the Associated Press introduced the first system for routinely transmitting **"wire photos,"** and thirty years later, in 1964, the Xerox Corporation introduced **long-distance xerography (LDX)**.

For many years, facsimile machines remained cumbersome, expensive, and difficult to operate, but in 1966, Xerox introduced the **Magnafax Telecopier**, a smaller, 46-pound facsimile machine that was easier to use and could be connected to any telephone line. Using this machine, a letter-sized document took about six minutes to transmit. The process was slow, but it represented a major technological step. In the late 1970s, Japanese companies entered the market, and soon a new generation of faster, smaller, and more efficient fax machines became available. Between 1973 and 1983, the number of fax machines in the United States increased from thirty thousand to three hundred thousand, but by 1989, the number jumped to four million. By the late 1980s, compact fax machines had revolutionized everyday communications around the world.

◆ The terrible carnage of World War I inspired British biologist Alexander Fleming to undertake a search that ultimately led to the discovery of an antibiotic that revolutionized medicine. Prior to his discovery of **penicillin**, the antiseptics and antibiotics that existed killed bacteria, but they destroyed human tissue as well. Because of this, they were useful only on surface wounds. In wartime, however, surface wounds were much less of a concern than more serious internal injuries.

Fleming was a bacteriologist when he volunteered for duty in the British Army's medical corps in 1914. He was horrified by the sight of so many men painfully enduring deep wounds crawling with bacteria and dismayed by his own inability to eradicate the germs without harming the wounded men. After the war, he returned to his laboratory, determined to find a more effective antibiotic. He theorized that the answer lay in fighting the invading organisms not with a caustic chemical that also harmed the patient but with an organic substance. He also believed that substances or secretions found in the human body held the key. By 1921, this line of inquiry led him to **lysozyme**, a secretion from human tears that proved successful against some bacteria but not against the most dangerous ones such as *Staphylococcus*, *Streptococcus*, and *Neisseria gonorrhoeae*.

Fleming continued his experiments with various organic substances that he cultured in small glass petri dishes in his laboratory. Occasionally, these dishes would become infected with mold spores and bacteria that naturally existed in the air, and Fleming would have to clean out the dishes and start over. One day in 1928, however, he noticed that in one dish containing *Staphylococcus*, the bacteria had been attacked by a

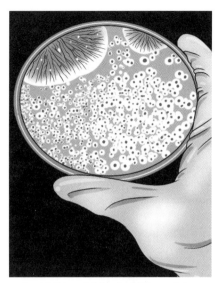

A petri dish containing *Penicillium notatum*

particular mold. He began studying this mold and discovered that it dissolved nearly every bacterium with which it came in contact. This mold, *Penicillium notatum*, led to penicillin, the heretofore elusive antibiotic.

Fleming spent the next decade exploring ways to mass produce penicillin and trying to overcome its tendency to degenerate within a few hours of being isolated from the mold. When World War II began, a massive effort was launched in both England and the United States to develop a durable penicillin that could be used in large quantities. In 1943, the U.S. Northern Regional Research Laboratory in Peoria, Illinois, isolated *Penicillium chrysogenum* from a moldy melon and solved the perplexing problem. Within a year, penicillin was saving thousands of lives on battlefields and around the world. By 1945, it was available on the civilian market, having completely revolutionized the treatment of disease. In that same year, Sir Alexander Fleming and two of his colleagues were awarded the Nobel Prize in Physiology or Medicine.

The **jet engine**, which is the standard propulsion system for all modern high-performance aircraft, was the invention of British test pilot and Royal Air Force officer Sir Frank Whittle. In 1928, Whittle envisioned an engine in which thrust would be generated by burning fuel in a combustion chamber. Air would be forced into the chamber ahead of the engine by a turbine. The thrust of the hot gas ejected from the rear of the turbojet engine would be greater than the flow of air in the front of the engine, and this, Whittle calculated, would generate forward motion.

The Heinkel He 178

Whittle patented his turbojet idea in 1930, but it was not then applied to actually propelling an aircraft in flight. Meanwhile in Germany, Hans Joachim Pabst von Ohain patented a similar idea in 1936. Then, a month after Whittle formed PowerJets, a company to build jet aircraft, the German aircraft company Heinkel began work on developing von Ohain's turbojet. Whittle completed his first engine in 1937 but deemed it not "flight ready," so von Ohain was the first to see his dream come true. On August 27, 1939, in Marienehe, Germany, the **Heinkel He 178** became the first jet aircraft to be flown. It flew with von Ohain's **HeS 3B engine**, the world's first practical turbojet.

In Italy, an entirely different type of jet engine was being developed in which an air compressor driven by a piston engine was used instead of a turbine. The **Caproni Campini N-1** was successfully flown with this engine on August 28, 1940, but was still slower than propeller-driven aircraft, so the idea was abandoned.

The first twin-jet aircraft, the **Heinkel He 280**, made its maiden flight on April 2, 1941. Frank Whittle's first successful engine made its initial flight on May 15, 1941, in the **Gloster E.28/29**. The first American jet aircraft, the **Bell XP-59 Airacomet**, which debuted on October 3, 1942, was powered by a Whittle turbojet.

The dawn of jet propulsion coincided with World War II, so the first jet aircraft to go into operational service was Germany's **Messerschmitt Me 262**, a two-engine fighter that made its maiden flight on July 18, 1942, and entered squadron service in June 1944. The first operational American jet fighter, the **Lockheed P-80 Shooting Star**, flew on January 8, 1944, and was followed four days later by the first operational British jet fighter, the **Gloster Meteor**. Neither the British nor the American aircraft actually saw combat in World War II.

The first **jetliner**, or jet-powered airliner, was the British **de Havilland DH 106 Comet**, which first flew on July 27, 1949. It was plagued by severe structural problems and was only marginally successful. The first entirely successful jetliner—and the one that marked the dawn of air travel as we have known it since the 1960s—was the American **Boeing 707**, whose 367–80 prototype flew on July 15, 1954, and which entered scheduled airline service with Pan American World Airways (Pan Am) on October 27, 1958.

Black-and-white photography (see no. 38) requires only sensitivity to light, but **color photography** is much more complex because it requires a separate sensitivity to each of several colors—for example, red, blue, and green—of the spectrum. In 1849, Alexandre-Edmond Becquerel in France is said to have succeeded in photographing the color spectrum but was unable to retain a permanent image.

A decade later, noted English physicist James Clerk Maxwell began to theorize about color photography, and in 1861, he demonstrated a system of color photography that involved photographing the same object with black-and-white film three times through a green, blue, and red filter. The resulting color image was produced by projecting the three photographs over one another on a screen using colored lights. The result was indeed a full-color photographic image, but it could not be fixed on paper and the process was practical only with immobile objects. Still, Maxwell's demonstration pointed the way.

In France, Auguste and Louis Lumière, Louis Ducos du Hauron, and Rodolphe Berthon conducted experiments in the first decade of the twentieth century that also used three black-and-white photographs to simulate color. Also in France in 1900, Georges Méliès and Charles Pathé used a mechanical stencil to create a precursor to color motion pictures. In 1912, German chemist Hans Fischer discovered that just as the silver compounds in black-and-white film reacted to light, other chemicals responded differently to various colored lights.

In the United States, Helmut Kalmus founded the Technicolor Laboratory at the Massachusetts Institute of Technology (MIT) in Cambridge, Massachusetts. His process utilized a film that was multilayered, with each layer sensitive to a different color. He first produced a two-color motion picture film that was used in 1917. At the same time, the Eastman Kodak Company was experimenting with various color processes using filters similar to the ones in Maxwell's demonstration fifty years earlier. In 1932, Technicolor technology succeeded in creating the first actual full-color motion picture film, which was used for Walt Disney's animated short *Flowers and Trees* in that same year. The first full-length, Technicolor-based feature was *Becky Sharp* (1935).

In 1935, the first practical full-color film for still photography—a **positive transparency film**—was developed by Leopold Mannes and Leopold Godowsky and licensed to Kodak. Marketed under the name **Kodachrome**, it remained the industry standard for over sixty years.

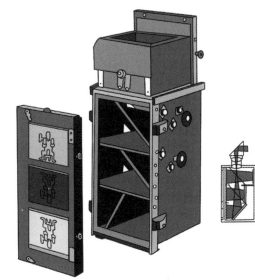

◆ Radar was initially an acronym coined in 1940 for **radio detection and ranging**, which explains how the technology functions. Radar is a system for detecting a distant object by transmitting high frequency radio waves, or **microwaves**, which "bounce," or echo, back to a receiver when they come in contact with an object. A characteristic of such high frequency radio waves is that they sharply reflect off metal and other non-absorbent materials. Ranging, or gauging the distance of the object, is accomplished by measuring the amount of time that it takes for the radio waves to reach an object and echo back to the receiver. Radar is commonly used to locate and track airplanes that are too far away to be tracked with the naked eye.

The principle underlying radar was first discovered in Germany by Heinrich Hertz in 1888, and in 1900, Nikola Tesla was the first person to describe a system of determining the location of a moving object using radio waves. In 1904, Christian Hülsmeyer patented a **radio detector** based on Tesla's idea. In the 1920s, Gregory Breit and Merle Tuve in the United States used a similar system to measure the depth of the ionosphere, the layer of the Earth's atmosphere that reflects radio waves.

The first practical radar for use in the detection of airplanes was developed by Scottish physicist Sir Robert Alexander Watson-Watt of the British National Physical Laboratory. By 1936, his installation at a secret military site at Bawdsey Manor on England's eastern coast could detect airplanes at altitudes up to 1,500 feet and at distances up to 75 miles. Perceiving the practical value of such a system for wartime use, the British government spent several million pounds to develop a workable system, and by the time World War II began in 1939, Watson-Watt's radar network could detect aircraft at 10,000 feet and 100 miles away.

During the Battle of Britain in 1940, radar was still top secret and played a crucial role in saving Britain from defeat by the German Air Force. In Germany, Rudolf Kühnhold at Telefunken in Würzburg had actually made major progress in radar in 1938, but further development was halted because German dictator Adolf Hitler believed that the field of electronics was too dominated by Jewish scientists. German radar research resumed in 1943, when the success of British radar technology became apparent, but by that time, British and American systems were much more highly refined.

Today, radar is an essential part of **air traffic control** at airports everywhere and is installed in all commercial and military aircraft.

In April 1938, Roy T. Plunkett was a research chemist with E. I. DuPont de Nemours & Company when he discovered **polytetrafluoroethylene (PTFE) resin**. He found the PTFE resin to be resistant to acids, exceptionally durable, and excellent as electrical insulator. Marketed under the name **Teflon**, PTFE resin was used to make pipes for corrosive materials, insulators, and pump gaskets.

In December 1954, two French engineers, Louis Hartman and Marc Grégoire, discovered that burned food would not stick to the inside of a frying pan that had been coated with Teflon. The discovery revolutionized the lives of cooks everywhere. In 1961, the first U.S.-manufactured Teflon coated pan, marketed as "The Happy Pan," went on sale. Today, Teflon is used in many common household products created by hundreds of manufacturers all over the world.

An advertisement for "The Happy Pan"

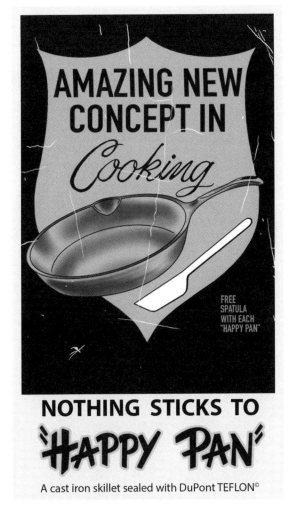

A cast iron skillet sealed with DuPont TEFLON©

Between the invention of the first practical typewriter in 1867 and the advent of practical fax machines 120 years later, no machine or process revolutionized the workplaces of business and industry more than **xerography**. The name was adapted from the Greek *xeros* meaning "dry" and *graph* meaning "to write" by the inventor of the process, American physicist Chester Floyd Carlson. Carlson arrived at his invention through studying a theory first put forth by Hungarian scientist Pál Selényi. Carlson's system used light, heat, and electricity to affix a dry, powdered pigment to paper.

Carlson subsequently perfected this process and produced his first xerographic copy on October 22, 1938. Amazingly, after he patented the process, he was unable to find a company willing to exploit the immense potential of his invention.

In 1944, Carlson finally signed an agreement with the Battelle Memorial Institute, a small, nonprofit scientific foundation in Columbus, Ohio, to develop the process further. In 1947 Battelle licensed Carlson's invention to a small firm called Haloid, which later changed its name to Xerox Corporation. The first automatic office copier that used ordinary paper was the **Xerox 914**, which was introduced in 1959. It produced seven copies a minute.

The **helicopter** is similar to an airplane in that it is a heavier-than-air aircraft, but unlike an airplane, it can take off vertically and is supported in the air, not by wings but by a large-diameter rotor driven by a vertical shaft. Helicopters can also move forward, backward, and sideways by continuously varying the pitch, or angle of attack, of the rotor blades.

The first functional helicopter design was drawn by Leonardo da Vinci in 1499, but he did not have the means to power his invention, and it could not have actually flown. The same was true of Sir George Cayley's design. In 1877, Italian inventor Enrico Forlianini built an unmanned steam helicopter that climbed 40 feet and flew for twenty seconds. On September 19, 1907, Louis-Charles Breguet and his brother Jacques of France flew for twenty seconds in their **gyroplane**, thus achieving the first manned helicopter flight. However, the machine was totally uncontrolled. Their colleague, Paul Cornu, accomplished a similar feat with his helicopter two months later, and on January 11, 1922, Marquis Raúl Pateras Pescara de Castelluccio flew his helicopter for a minute in Paris.

In Madrid, Spain, on January 9, 1923, Juan de la Cierva first flew his **autogiro**, a craft that was a cross between an airplane and a true helicopter. It had a conventional engine and propeller to generate forward motion, but the airflow produced by the forward motion rotated a large-diameter, unpowered rotor, which provided lift. Cierva was able to fly for 2.5 miles at a height of 80 feet on his first flight.

French engineer Étienne Œhmichen was perhaps the first to achieve a sustained, controlled flight in a helicopter. On May 1, 1923, he flew his **four-rotor helicopter** for about 400 feet in a straight line, turned, and

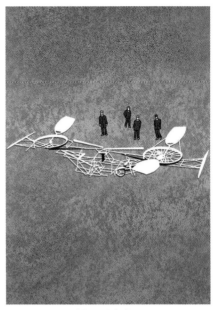

Paul Cornu's helicopter

flew back. On May 4, 1924, Œhmichen flew .062 miles in just under eight minutes, but problems of stability and control plagued helicopter designers. Cierva continued to improve his autogiro, while helicopter projects were carried out by Louis Breguet—who had built his first experimental helicopter in 1907—in France in 1935, and by Karl Focke and Gerd Achgelis in Germany in 1936.

A practical, controllable helicopter was finally built and flown in 1939 by Igor Sikorsky, a Russian-born aircraft designer who had emigrated to the United States after World War I. His **VS-300** was initially tested in tethered flight—meaning it was tied to the ground—in 1939, and on May 13, 1940, it flew freely for the first time. On May 6, 1941, Sikorsky flew the VS-300 for over 1 hour, 32.5 minutes. The success of the VS-300 led to the **Sikorsky R-4** and **R-5**, which entered production in 1942 and 1943, respectively, and saw service with the Allies in World War II as rescue helicopters.

The machines once known metaphorically as "electronic brains" revolutionized engineering and mathematics by extending the reach of the mind the way the automobile and airplane extended the reach of the body.

The first step toward the computer revolution was the development in 1679 of **binary notation**, the eventual basis for many computer languages. Philosopher and mathematician Gottfried Wilhelm von Leibniz developed a system whereby all numbers could be noted as either 1 or 0. Although there was no application for his system in 1679, in computers, 1 and 0 can be expressed as either an open or closed circuit, a pair of magnetic states, or many other opposite conditions. Contemporary computers operate on billions of 1's and 0's in a fraction of a second.

The first people to apply electricity to binary notation were the French engineers T. Abraham and E. Bloch in 1918. A year later, W. H. Eccles and F. W. Jordan in England built a machine based on the same principle.

In 1937, American engineer Howard Aiken designed the **IBM Mark 7**, the grandfather of today's **mainframe computers**. A massive machine standing 8 feet (2.4 meters) high and 50 feet long, the Mark 7 used vacuum tubes and had electromechanical rather than electronic switches.

The first truly **electronic computers** were developed several years later, prompted by the technological needs of World War II. There was a great deal of independent work done both in the United States and Britain, but the first electronic computer was **Colossus I**, built in 1941 for the British government at the University of Manchester by Alan Turing and M. H. A. Neuman. It helped to crack Germany's secret **Ultra code**, and by 1943, it was breaking Axis codes on a daily basis. Colossus was followed in 1942 by the 30-ton (27 metric ton) **Electronic Numerical Integrator and Computer** developed for the U.S. government by John Mauchly and John Presper Eckert at the University of Pennsylvania. ENIAC, which did not become fully operational until 1946, was a thousand times faster than the prewar IBM Mark 7, but its eighteen thousand vacuum tubes caused frequent downtime.

The first electronic computer with stored memory was the **IBM Selective Sequence Electronic Calculator (SSEC)**, developed by Frank Hamilton and introduced in 1948. The first commercially successful electronic computer, the **Sperry Universal Automatic Computer (UNIVAC)**, was designed by Eckert and Mauchly and introduced in 1951. The **IBM 1401**, marketed in 1959, was the first computer that replaced mechanical business machines in large numbers in business and industry.

The **transistorized computer**, in which solid-state transistors replaced cumbersome and fragile vacuum tubes, was designed in 1958 by Seymour Cray for Control Data Corporation. This was the predecessor of a generation of solid-state processors that were vastly smaller and faster than anything that could have been imagined even a few years before.

Cray later formed his own company and went on to develop a series of cutting-edge supercomputers. The **Cray 1** supercomputer, introduced in 1975, was capable of 100 million operations per second. In 1985, this model was superseded by the **Cray 2**, which was capable of 1.2 billion operations per second.

The theory of nuclear energy was first advanced by the renowned physicist Albert Einstein in his **theory of relativity** (1905), in which he stated that energy was equal to mass at the speed of light ($E = mc^2$). In other words, mass could be converted into energy if it were propelled at the speed of light. Einstein's hypothesis remained in the realm of the theoretical until 1938, when three German scientists—Otto Hahn, Lise Meitner, and Fritz Strassman—discovered that uranium, when bombarded by neutrons, broke down into barium and krypton, and released tremendous quantities of heat in a process known as **nuclear fission**.

Danish physicist Niels Henrik David Bohr, learning of these experiments, realized the potential of using the process to create a military explosive, or **atomic bomb**, and he traveled to the United States to urge Americans to undertake the development of such a weapon before the Germans did. Ironically, the development of atomic energy in Germany was actually ahead of

similar work in America. This could have led to nuclear weapons in the early 1940s had leading German scientists not emigrated or been forced out of their profession because they were Jewish.

The first **nuclear reactor**, or device built to contain a self-sustaining nuclear chain reaction, was constructed on a squash court beneath the bleachers at Stagg Field at the University of Chicago, under the direction of the Italian physicist Enrico Fermi. Fermi, who had won the 1938 Nobel Prize in Physics for his work in neutron physics, had theorized that a nuclear chain reaction was possible. The Chicago reactor contained 50 tons of cadmium control rods and 500 tons of graphite, the latter to slow down the world's first controlled nuclear chain reaction, which was initiated on December 2, 1942. The U.S. Army's Manhattan Engineering District underwrote the construction of the reactor as a first step toward the development of a full-scale nuclear weapon (see no. 80).

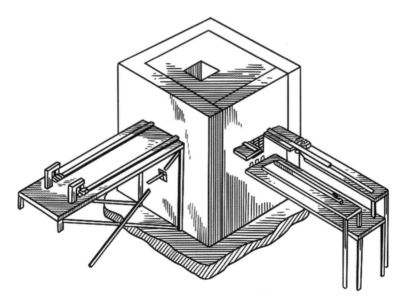

Schematic of the first nuclear reactor

The massive potential power of **nuclear weapons** was first theorized in 1938 from the work of Otto Hahn, Lise Meitner, and Fritz Strassman of Germany (see no. 79). Believing that Germany was engaged in a program to develop such weapons, Danish physicist Niels Henrik David Bohr, who emigrated to the United States on the eve of World War II in 1939, told expatriate Hungarian physicist Leo Szilard about the work being done in Germany. Szilard approached Albert Einstein, whose theory had opened the door to **nuclear fission**, and asked him to write a letter to President Franklin D. Roosevelt detailing the danger of inaction and recommending that the United States be the first to undertake the development of an **atomic bomb**. Roosevelt made the decision to build the bomb and assigned the project to the Manhattan District of the U.S. Army Corps of Engineers under the command of Major General Leslie R. Groves. The **Manhattan Project** became one of the most top secret—and expensive—projects in American history.

In 1942, Enrico Fermi initiated the world's first controlled **nuclear chain reaction** at the University of Chicago, using **uranium-235** as the fissionable material. At the same time, scientists working with the **cyclotron**—a **particle accelerator**—at the University of California, Berkeley discovered that **plutonium-239** was also potentially fissionable. The Corps of Engineers set up a secret uranium-235 factory in Oak Ridge, Tennessee, and a plutonium-239 plant in Hanford, Washington.

Meanwhile, the Manhattan Project was relocated to a remote site near Los Alamos, New Mexico, where Szilard and Fermi were joined by Arthur H. Compton of the University of Chicago, J. Robert Oppenheimer of the University of California, Berkeley, and a team of many other chemists, physicists, and engineers.

The first nuclear weapon, a uranium-235 bomb, was detonated at a site code-named "Trinity" in the New Mexico desert on July 16, 1945. The next two weapons consisted of a uranium-235 bomb, which was dropped on the Japanese city of Hiroshima on August 6, and a plutonium-239 bomb, which was dropped on Nagasaki on August 9. The explosions brought World War II to an abrupt halt.

Concurrent nuclear weapons projects in Japan and Germany had failed to produce operational bombs. Working in part with data stolen from the United States, the Soviet Union became the world's second nuclear power in 1949.

All **electromagnetic energy** can be characterized as waves with a specific wavelength and frequency distributed over a continuous range known as the **electromagnetic spectrum**. For example, some radio waves have a wavelength of 6 feet and a frequency of 50 million hertz (Hz-cycles per second). Visible light waves have a wavelength of 400 to 700 millimicrons, and typical X-rays have a length of 0.01 millimicrons and a frequency of 30×10^{12} millions. **Microwaves** (**short waves** or **high frequency radio waves**) are the shortest of radio waves, with a length of 0.1 millimeter and a frequency of 3×10^9 Hz. They are found in the non-ionizing portion of the energy spectrum, between radio waves and visible light. "Non-ionizing" means that microwaves do not detach charged particles or produce atoms with an unbalanced plus or minus charge. Microwaves can therefore safely produce heat and not cause food to become radioactive. Microwaves are reflected from most metals, but they produce inductive resonances in the atoms of many other substances. In fact, it was the discovery of their reaction to metals that led to the invention of radar (see no. 74). It was their ability to produce resonant coupling that led to the invention of the **microwave oven**.

The idea of using microwave energy to cook food was accidentally discovered by Percy LeBaron Spencer of the Raytheon Company when he found that radar waves had melted a candy bar in his pocket. Experiments showed that microwave heating could raise the internal temperature of many foods far more rapidly than a conventional oven. The first Raytheon commercial microwave oven was the **1161 Radarange**, which was marketed in 1955. Rated at 1600 watts, it was so large and so expensive that it was practical only for restaurant and institutional use.

In 1967, Amana, a division of Raytheon, introduced its domestic **Radarange** microwave oven, marking the beginning of the use of microwave ovens in home kitchens. Although sales were slow during the first few years—partially due to the oven's relatively expensive price tag—the concept of quick microwave cooking had arrived. In succeeding years, Litton and a number of other companies joined the countertop microwave oven market. By the end of 1971, the price of countertop units began to decrease, and their capabilities were expanded.

A unique material for fastening objects together, **Velcro** was invented in 1948 by Swiss engineer George de Mestral who noticed that burrs, or burdock seeds, had many tiny, stiff, hook-like protrusions that made them stick firmly to clothing or animal hair. He decided to apply the same principle to a fastening system for clothes that would be easier than buttons.

He called his invention, which was patented in 1957, **Velcro brand hook-and-loop fastener**, from the French *velours* meaning "velvet" and *crochet* meaning "hook." His new fastener consisted of two strips of nylon: one with small, rigid hooks and the other with pliable loops to create a remarkably simple yet efficient fastener. Although originally designed for textiles, Velcro is used for a myriad of fastening jobs across many different situations and industries, including healthcare, transportation, military, aircraft, spacecraft, and more. The word "Velcro" is a registered trademark of the firm of the same name.

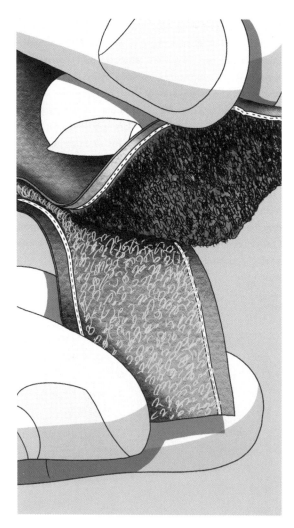

The first sustained **nuclear reaction** was achieved in 1942, and the first application of nuclear energy was in weapons to help win World War II. After the war, **nuclear energy** seemed to be a promising source of unlimited, low-cost electrical energy for civilian use.

A nuclear reaction creates intense heat that can be used to produce steam, which turns turbines and produces electricity. The world's first power-generating **nuclear reactor** was the **experimental breeder reactor**, known commonly as the **EBR**, developed in America at the Argonne National Laboratory. It began producing electricity on December 20, 1951. The second reactor to go online was the **homogeneous reactor experiment**, known commonly as the **HRE**, at the Oak Ridge National Laboratory on February 24, 1953. Today, there more than four hundred commercial **nuclear power plants** operating in over thirty countries around the world, a quarter of which is in the United States, and another quarter is divided between France and Russia. In Belgium, France, and South Korea, nuclear power produces over half of the national requirements for electricity (see no. 79 and no. 29).

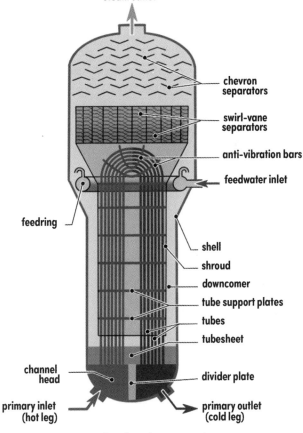

A nuclear steam generator

Light waves typically travel in a straight line, but **optical fibers** permit the bending of light. An optical fiber is a flexible glass or transparent plastic filament that transmits light via a series of internal reflections.

Although this concept was first discovered in 1870 by John Tyndall, an English physicist, the first practical use occurred in 1955, when Indian American scientist Narinder Singh Kapany incorporated **fiber optics** in an **endoscope**, an optical instrument used by doctors for examining inside the human body.

In 1960, the Corning Glass company developed extremely pure glass, which permitted the transmission of light and other energy over great distances. Since the 1970s, fiber optics have been used to transmit telex, telephone, and cable television signals much more efficiently than was ever possible with metal wire. In addition to their use in communication, they are also used in endoscopy. Fiber optics have revolutionized medical endoscopy procedures and made many other medical and surgical procedures less invasive than before.

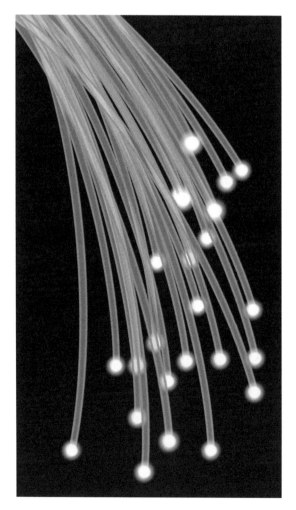

Practical television transmission became a reality in 1927 and was in common use by 1950. Magnetic recording of sound also became a reality during the same period, so it was natural to seek a way of recording television pictures by a means other than motion picture film. Experiments were first conducted in the late 1940s, and the 3M Company, which manufactures Scotch brand tape, demonstrated the first **videotape recorder** in 1951. RCA introduced a competing process in 1954, but neither system was totally satisfactory. In 1951, Alexander M. Poniatoff, founder of the California-based Ampex Corporation, began working on the development of a practical machine with Charles Ginsberg, Charles Anderson, and a young student named Ray Dolby, who in 1967, invented the **Dolby** system of noise reduction in magnetic recording. On March 2, 1955, these men introduced a four-head, grooved-drum system that still stands as the first ever practical videotape recorder. After improvements, it was marketed in April 1956 as the **VR 1000**. On November 30, 1956, CBS broadcast the first videotaped television program in California, the *CBS Evening News with Douglas Edwards*, which had been recorded three hours earlier in New York. At the same time, 3M began manufacturing Scotch videotape for use in the Ampex machine. The first **color videotape recorder**, the **Ampex VR 1000B**, was introduced in 1958. A transistorized version went on the market in 1963.

Having initially opened the field, Ampex failed to develop the enormous potential of this burgeoning market, which eventually came to be dominated by Japanese companies such as Hitachi, JVC, Matsushita, and along with Philips in the Netherlands. Both Sony and Philips introduced home video recorders in 1964. In 1970, Philips introduced **videocassettes** and began to market **VCRs (videocassette recorders)** in April 1972. Sony also marketed a camera with a compact cassette called **Beta** in 1982. The **VHS standard cassette** was introduced the same year. By the end of the 1980s, however, the VHS format had all but eliminated popular use of Sony's Beta format and became the preferred mode of watching and creating video until the rise of the DVD (digital video disc) in the late 1990s and 2000s.

power source

100% mirror

quartz flash lamp

ruby crystal

switch

polished aluminum cylinder

95% mirror

laser beam

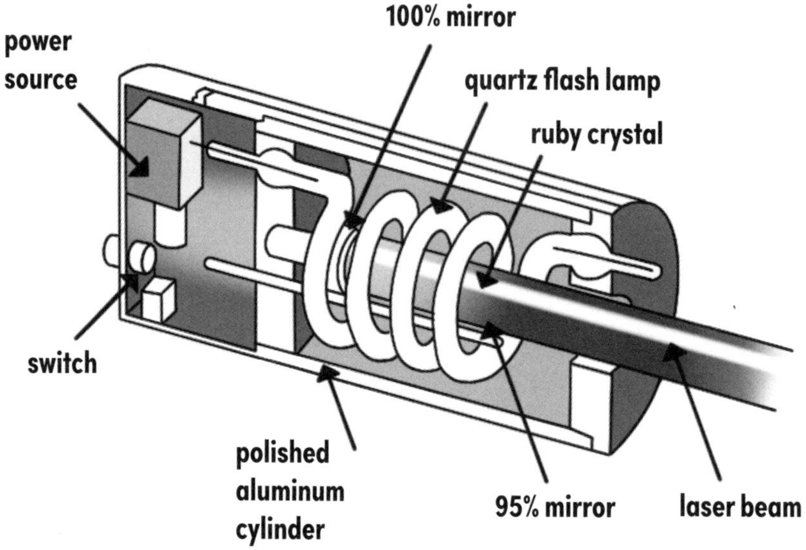

LASER is an acronym for **light amplification by stimulated emission of radiation**. The basic description offers few clues to the vast array of applications of "amplified light," which range from a means of reading compact discs to employment as a cutting tool in microsurgery.

Albert Einstein theorized in 1917 that if there were more photons than electrons in a form of radiation, such as light, the energy difference could stimulate an electron to jump to a lower energy level, causing the emission of another photon, hence amplification.

In 1951, American physicist Charles Hard Townes, who would later go on to win the 1964 Nobel Prize in Physics, described a similar system using microwaves instead of light.

In 1955 he built a demonstration **MASER**, which used microwaves as the energy to be amplified. In 1957, Gordon Gould of Columbia University described an optical system using light—the laser. Gould later said his initial ideas for the laser "came in a flash" one night, which he proceeded to write down in a notebook he titled *Some Rough Calculations on the Feasibility of a Laser*. Gould, however, did not file for a patent until 1959 after other similar designs had been filed, and his patent was not issued until 1977.

The first **ruby laser**, in which lasing takes place in a solid rod of the mineral corundum, was built in 1960 by Theodore H. Maiman at the Hughes Research Laboratory in California. The **helium neon gas laser** was developed in 1961.

In the late nineteenth century, science fiction writers such as Jules Verne inspired and intrigued the public with stories of human beings flying, not just into the air, but into outer space. Until the middle of the twentieth century, most people assumed that it was highly improbable that anyone would ever actually travel in space as the practical problems of escaping Earth's gravity and supporting human life in outer space seemed insurmountable.

However, the tremendous technological advances that occurred during World War II changed everything. The most notable development during this era was the **V-2 rocket**, which was designed in Germany by Dr. Wernher von Braun. After Germany's defeat, V-2 technology was captured both by the United States and the former Soviet Union and used it as the basis of independent rocket programs in both countries (see no. 23).

In 1957, the Soviet Union succeeded in launching **Sputnik 1**, the first object made on Earth to be placed in orbit around the Earth. This was the first step in achieving the dream of carrying human beings into outer space. The launch of *Sputnik 1* also initiated a politically inspired "space race" between the United States and the Soviet Union, with the obvious goal of being the first nation to launch one of its own citizens into orbit in outer space.

Over the next four years, both countries launched unmanned spacecraft, including some that were rehearsals for manned missions. Finally, on April 12, 1961, the Soviet Union launched *Vostok 1,* piloted by Yuri A. Gagarin. The first human in space completed one orbit of the Earth before returning to a hero's welcome. The first American in space, Alan B. Shepard, made his flight only three weeks later on May 5. By the end of 1961, two Soviet cosmonauts and two American astronauts had flown in space, but the Americans did not actually orbit the Earth. The first American to orbit the Earth was John Glenn on February 20, 1962. Within the first five years after Gagarin's flight, the Soviets had conducted eight manned space flights and the Americans had flown twelve.

In December 1968, the United States' **Apollo 8**—carrying Frank Borman, James Lovell, and William Anders on board—became the first manned space flight to leave Earth's orbit and fly into deep space (see no. 87). The first Soviet woman in space was Valentina Tereshkova, who was launched for forty-eight orbits aboard **Vostok 6** on June 14, 1963. The first American woman in space was Sally Ride, who flew a six-day mission aboard the **space shuttle orbiter Challenger** in June 1983.

The International Space Station

Communications satellites have greatly impacted our lives by making instantaneous global communications both possible and reasonably inexpensive. Today, telephone, television, and other transmissions are routinely carried by a huge network of communication satellites in **geostationary orbits** around the Earth.[1]

Although the process of bouncing **high frequency radio waves**, or **microwaves**, off objects in space to facilitate long-distance communication was envisioned by the English engineer and science fiction writer Arthur C. Clarke in 1945, the first satellite was not launched until 1957. The first ever communications satellite was the U.S. Army's **Signal Communication by Orbiting Relay Equipment (SCORE)**, launched on December 18, 1958. Among other things, it helped to broadcast a Christmas greeting from President Dwight Eisenhower. Both the United States and the Soviet Union developed and launched numerous types of military communication satellites over the next several years, but the first commercial communications satellite was *Telstar 1*, built by Bell Laboratories for their parent company, AT&T, and launched by NASA on July 10, 1962. *Telstar 1* was a 175-pound craft with 1,064 transmitters.

In 1965, the American Communications Satellite Corporation (COMSAT), in cooperation with the International Telecommunications Satellite Consortium (INTELSAT) began launching a series of communications satellites as initial building blocks in the global network of international communications satellites. The first, designated *Intelsat 1-F1* and known commonly

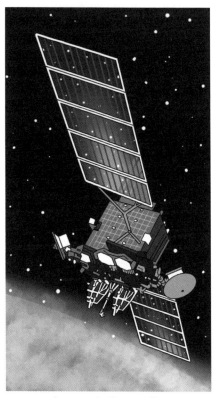

A communications satellite

as "Early Bird," was launched on April 6, 1965. INTELSAT launches continued into the 1980s. Meanwhile, COMSAT launched a series of Comstar communications satellites for domestic use by AT&T and General Telephone & Electronics (GTE). *Comstar 1* was launched on May 13, 1976.

---

1   A geostationary orbit is one in which the satellite orbits in the same direction as the Earth's rotation, but at a higher speed, therefore appearing to be stationary, i.e., remaining over the same point on Earth.

Humans have long fantasized about visiting our neighboring planets. By the middle of the twentieth century, technology had evolved to the point where this was possible with remote-control robots known collectively as **interplanetary spacecraft**.

Interplanetary spacecraft, like spacecraft designed to operate within Earth's atmosphere, are launched into space by rockets powerful enough to lift them out of the Earth's gravitational field. They consist of seven major components:

NASA's *Mariner* 10 spacecraft

1. A primary booster.
2. A secondary rocket to carry them past the gravitational influence of Earth and beyond into deep space.
3. Small thruster rockets to maneuver the spacecraft in space.
4. A power source, which includes solar panels for use as far out as Mars or a radioisotope generator for use on deeper space flights. (The decay of radioisotopes generates heat energy that can be converted to electricity.)
5. Cameras and scientific sensors to gather data about the planet being studied.
6. An "uplink" antenna to receive instructions from Earth.
7. A "downlink" antenna to send information back to Earth. Some are equipped with a landing module designed to travel to the surface of another planet.

The Moon, a satellite of Earth and not a planet, was the first space destination. In 1959, the Soviet *Luna 3* spacecraft photographed the far side of the Moon not visible from Earth for the first time, and between 1966 and 1968, a series of unmanned American **lunar orbiter** and **surveyor** spacecraft landed on and mapped most of the Moon to analyze its surface closely.

On December 14, 1962, the American *Mariner 2* that had launched toward Venus four months earlier became the first spacecraft to fly past and photograph another planet close up. On July 14, 1965, *Mariner 4* arrived at and photographed the surface of Mars. Seven years later, *Mariner 9* was placed into orbit around Mars for ninety days. During the late 1960s, the Soviet Union and the United States sent additional probes to the Moon, Mars, and Venus, and the Americans sent a dozen humans to the Moon.

In the early 1970s, the emphasis shifted to exploration of more distant planets and actually reaching the surface of the planets. *Mariner 10* was the first spacecraft ever sent to the planet Mercury, and it conducted three flybys between March 29, 1974, and March 24, 1975.

To explore the larger outer planets, the United States launched two pairs of spacecraft. *Pioneer 10* was launched on March 3, 1972, becoming the first spacecraft to fly by Jupiter on December 3, 1973. *Pioneer 11* launched on April 6, 1973, reaching Jupiter on December 2, 1974. It became the first spacecraft to fly by Saturn on September 1, 1979. The *Voyager 2* spacecraft that launched in 1977 afforded even more remarkable views of the outer planets and became the first spacecraft to visit Uranus in 1986 and Neptune in 1989. The first flyby of Pluto was performed by *New Horizons* in 2015—eleven years after its initial launch in 2006.

In the early 1970s, the daily lives of people throughout the developed world were changed profoundly by the advent of a small electronic machine that could perform basic mathematical problems much more quickly and more accurately than they could be worked out on paper. **Calculators** expanded the math capabilities of everyone from high school students to salespeople and executives.

The original compact calculator was the abacus, developed in China in the ninth century (see no. 9). The young French mathematician Blaise Pascal invented the first **adding machine** in 1642, a clever device driven by gears and capable of performing mechanical addition and subtraction. The first commercially successful adding machine was developed in 1886 by William Seward Burroughs. The **Millionaire**, a machine invented by Otto Steiger in 1894, was the first adding machine also capable of direct multiplication.

The **handheld pocket calculator** was invented at Texas Instruments, Incorporated (TI) in 1967 by a development team that included Jerry D. Merryman, James H. Van Tassel and Jack St. Clair Kilby. In 1958, Kilby invented the **microchip**, a multiple transistor instrument that was a miniaturized electronic circuit destined to become an essential element not only in handheld calculators but in the computer revolution as well.

The pocket calculator went on the market on September 21, 1972, as the **TI-2500** and was capable of addition, subtraction, multiplication, and division. It had a floating decimal point and an eight-digit, **light-emitting diode (LED)** display. The TI-2500 measured 5.5 × 3 × 1.7 inches and weighed 12 ounces. The original TI-2500 retailed for $120, but within a few years, equivalent machines were retailing for under $10. Today, it is hard to imagine life without this handy invention.

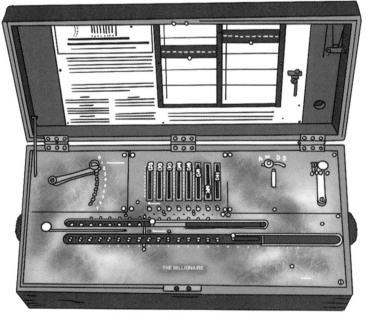

Otto Steiger's Millionaire calculator

Space flight, especially involving placing human beings in space, has been one of the most complex scientific and technological efforts undertaken in the twentieth century. The project that ultimately landed humans on the surface of the Moon brought together elements of many scientific and technological disciplines to solve the most difficult engineering challenge in history.

The first Earth-orbiting spacecraft, **Sputnik 1**, was launched by the Soviet Union (USSR; now Russia and neighboring countries) in 1957, and the first human beings traveled into space. Having achieved the dream of successfully supporting human life in outer space in 1961, both the United States and the Soviet Union committed themselves to sending one of their citizens to the Moon and back. Although the details of the Soviet effort remained shrouded in secrecy for nearly three decades, the American project was highly publicized. By the mid-1960s, both nations had developed and successfully flown into space spacecraft capable of carrying more than one crew member—a development that was essential to mastering the complexities of flying to the Moon.

The design for the American lunar mission involved the *Apollo* spacecraft, which would carry a crew of three **astronauts** from the Earth to orbit around the Moon. Two members of the crew would then travel to the lunar surface, remain for several days and then rejoin their colleague for the return trip to Earth. The first manned Apollo spacecraft, **Apollo 7,** was test-flown in Earth's orbit in October 1968. On December 21, 1968, **Apollo 8** became the first manned spacecraft to fly to the Moon. On Christmas Eve, Frank Borman, James Covell, and William Anders became the first humans to orbit another world. No landing

was planned, and *Apollo 8* returned home safely.

Two further training flights followed in early 1969, and on July 16, 1969, **Apollo 11** was launched from the Kennedy Space Center in Florida, destined to take the first humans to the Moon. On July 20, Neil Armstrong and Edwin "Buzz" Aldrin left Michael Collins in lunar orbit and descended to the surface. A few hours later, Armstrong became the first human being to set foot on a world other than Earth.

Between November 1968 and December 1972, a total of six more *Apollo* spacecraft carrying two astronauts each made the three-day, quarter-million-mile journey from Earth to the Moon. An additional spacecraft, **Apollo 13**, experienced an in-flight emergency, preventing it from completing its mission of landing two more astronauts on the Moon.

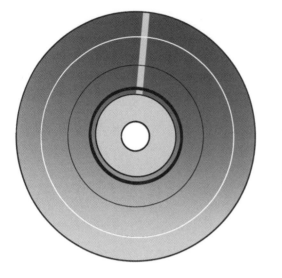

The **videodisc** is a means of storing and retrieving video images that was first introduced to the marketplace shortly after home videotape recording became popular. Videodiscs were first marketed by Philips of the Netherlands in 1972, and subsequently by Thomson-CSF in France, JVC in Japan, and RCA in the United States. The JVC system was the first to use an **optical tracking signal** linked to the video signal.

Videodisc technology differs from videotape technology in that its information is stored as a close-pitched spiral of optically readable micropits on a flat disc rather than in magnetic microdomains on tape and is read by a laser rather than a magnetic head. Another major difference is that home videotape players were also recorders. Videotape could be recorded on, whereas videodiscs were available only in prerecorded form. For this reason, videodiscs were not very popular when they were first introduced and did not enjoy large-scale consumer acceptance until the early 1990s, when buyers realized that their picture quality was far superior to that of videotape. In 1996, the DVD (digital video disc) was released, and because of the higher quality video, sound, lifespan, and interactive capabilities, it soon became the preferred format for video and rendered the VHS obsolete. The Blu-ray Disc, designed to compete with and succeed the DVD, was released in 2006, and was capable of storing hours of higher definition video. Demand for video discs significantly decreased however, with the rise of online video streaming services in the late 2010s.

◆ The **Voyager** program ranks as one of the greatest engineering feats in the history of technology. These spacecrafts followed **Pioneer 10** and **Pioneer 11** as the only probes to visit the outer planets and to travel into interstellar space.

The *Voyagers* were a pair of 1,800-pound machines that successfully traveled billions of miles to the four largest planets of the solar system, passing much closer to the planets than the *Pioneers* and tak-

Pioneer 10

ing thousands of photographs that changed our understanding of those distant worlds and their moons.

Voyager 2 was launched on August 20, 1977, followed by *Voyager 1* on September 5, 1977. *Voyager 1* reached Jupiter on March 5, 1979, and *Voyager 2* followed on July 9. They approached Saturn on November 12, 1980, and August 25, 1981, respectively. The pictures they transmitted showed the two largest planets and their moons in unprecedented detail.

After Saturn, *Voyager 1* turned north away from the flat plane on which the planets orbit the Sun in order to fly past Saturn's huge moon Titan. *Voyager 2*, meanwhile, continued onward, reaching Uranus on January 24, 1986, and Neptune on August 24, 1989. Because the orbit of Pluto was closer to the Earth than Neptune in 1989, the probe was really at the outermost planet in the solar system.

Before *Pioneers 10* and *11* and the *Voyagers*, no human-made craft had ever gone farther than 60 million miles from home. All four of these craft, however,

visited Jupiter, 400 million miles away, and *Voyager 2* transmitted photographs from 2.8 billion miles away. However, the wonder of these four goes beyond the extraordinary things they showed us about our own solar system. They were each designed to fly past a planet and continue traveling, and because there is no friction in space, these four will keep going past the edge of the solar system, and potentially continue forever.

Beyond the overlapping orbits of Neptune and Pluto lies the **heliopause**, which is defined as the place where the gravitational influence of the Sun—for which the Greek word is *helios*—becomes negligible to the point where the Sun is just another tiny star in the sky. This is the theoretical point where the solar system ends and interstellar space begins, between 3.4 and 4 billion miles away from the Sun. All four of these spacecrafts have now crossed into interstellar space. *Pioneer 10* was first to do so in 1985, and by 1992, both *Voyagers* were out of the solar system, moving at a speed of about 300 million miles a year.

At that rate, it will be more than seventy thousand years before one of these four will have gone as far as Alpha Centauri, the nearest star to our Sun. In fact, the *Pioneers* and *Voyagers* left the solar system several billion miles apart going in different directions and none is headed toward Alpha Centauri. *Pioneer 10*'s trajectory, however, will take it near the star Aldebaran in about eight million years.

Electrical calculating machines (see no. 90) have existed since the early twentieth century, and the early electronic computers that are the forerunners of modern computers date from 1941. However, **desktop computers**, which revolutionized our way of life, were not introduced until 1977.

The essential first step was the invention of the **microprocessor**, a machine that combines the equivalent of thousands of transistors onto a single, tiny silicon chip.

The IBM personal computer

The microprocessor was developed by Ted Hoff at Intel Corporation in 1971 in the Santa Clara Valley south of the San Francisco Bay Area of California, which was destined to become known to the world as **Silicon Valley** thanks to the microprocessor and computer industry that grew up there.

In 1976, in what is now the Silicon Valley, Steve Jobs and Steve Wozniak created a homemade microprocessor computer board called **Apple I**. Working from Jobs's parents' garage, the two men began to manufacture and market the Apple I to local hobbyists and electronics enthusiasts. In April of that year, Jobs and Wozniak founded Apple Computer, Inc., and in 1977, they introduced the Apple II as the world's first personal computer. Based on a board of their design, the Apple II, complete with a keyboard and color graphics, retailed for $1,290. By the end of 1978, Apple was one of the fastest-growing companies in the United States, and the **Apple II+**, with a twelvefold increase in memory, was next offered for sale.

The microcomputer revolution exploded in the late 1970s and early 1980s as Apple shipped tens of thousands of their inexpensive computers worldwide; the idea of a home computer became reality. Businesses and educational institutions that would never have been able to buy computers or train people to use the complex mainframe computer languages were now able to take advantage of this technology. Apple grew to a $500 million company in only five years, and it continued to dominate the industry until the giant IBM (Internal Business Machines) Corporation introduced its **personal computer (PC)** in August 1981. By the 1990s, Apple and IBM divided the market, and microcomputers had become a familiar fixture in businesses, schools, and homes throughout the industrialized world. Companies began developing new models and uses for personal computers quickly throughout the following decades, with each year bringing a faster, more compact, and better computer. Laptops became more common, and the PalmPilot, one of the first widely adopted handheld PDAs (personal digital assistants), was released in 1996. These developments, along with the growing ability to easily access the internet and increasing adoption of smartphones in the aughts soon made PCs central to life, work, and education in much of the world. In 2018, 92 percent of all households in the United States had at least one type of computer.

The most revolutionary innovation in mass market recorded music since the invention of the phonograph came about in 1979 through a blending of computer and laser technology. Although **compact disc (CD)** technology was developed independently by Sony in Japan and Philips in the Netherlands, the two companies collaborated in the final stages of the process in order to establish a worldwide standard that would benefit both corporations.

Almost from the moment that compact discs became commercially available in 1982, they began to take over the market dominated by traditional, grooved, vinyl long-playing records (LPs). By the 1990s, LPs had all but disappeared from music stores in North America and Europe as most new releases by major artists were simply no longer available on vinyl records.

The compact disc differed from vinyl in several ways. It was much smaller at 4.25 inches compared to 12 inches in diameter, and because the CD's laser makes no contact with the disc, a CD could withstand the wear and tear of repeated usage much longer than an LP. Furthermore, the sound quality of a CD could be improved because music was recorded digitally; that is, the sound is not physically scratched into or onto the surface as with a vinyl LP, but rather encoded into a reflective surface using the same kind of binary notation used in computer language. That notation is then "read" by a laser (see no. 86). Compact disc technology also made it possible to eliminate surface noise that often distracted LP listeners from the contents of the records.

By 2007, over 200 billion CDs had been sold around the world. However, sales began falling in the aughts and 2010s with the rise of digital music purchasing and streaming platforms like iTunes, Pandora, and Spotify.

In the 1950s, when crewed spacecraft were first seen as a real possibility, these vessels were conceived as vehicles that could be used again and again like airplanes. However, the objective of putting humans into space became the subject of a politically motivated "space race" between the United States and the Soviet Union (USSR; now Russia and neighboring nations). Both nations decided that the fastest way to accomplish this goal was to use **space capsules**. These could be launched into space on a rocket, re-enter the Earth's atmosphere after a mission, and be recovered after parachuting back to the Earth.

The space shuttle *Discovery*

Space capsules were of relatively simple design and were each intended for only a single space flight. Both the United States and the Soviet Union launched their first space capsules in 1961. The United States successfully launched thirty-one crewed capsules through 1975. The USSR continued using capsules, having launched nearly 100 missions by the early 1990s. In 2003, China became the third country ever to successfully launch a crewed spacecraft.

The first reusable crewed spacecraft ever built was the American Boeing **X-20 Dyna-Soar**. It was a single-pilot craft designed to be launched atop a *Titan* rocket, and it was equipped with wings for an airplane-like landing. The first of 10 *X-20s* was nearly complete when the project was canceled in 1963, so the spacecraft never actually flew in space.

The *X-20* was canceled because it was decided that space capsules could do the job of getting an astronaut into space just as well and could be developed more quickly, but when the United States ended its capsule program, the decision was made to develop a winged craft called a **space shuttle**. The name implied reusability, and a system that could be used many times without being discarded had many obvious advantages. The **Space Shuttle Transportation System (STS)** included a winged spacecraft, called an orbiter, mounted on a huge fuel tank, which was launched using its own engines, as well as two massive solid rocket boosters (SRB) attached to the tank.

The first STS mission was flown by the orbiter *Columbia*, which was launched on April 12, 1981. This flight lasted four days, but subsequent missions averaged seven days and lasted up to eleven days. There had been twenty-four successful missions when the orbiter *Challenger* was lost in a fatal accident shortly after being launched on January 28, 1986. Flights resumed on September 29, 1988 and continued until NASA's retirement of the last space shuttle orbiter, *Atlantis*, in 2011, after launching a total of 135 space shuttle missions, and the construction of the International Space Station. In 2020, NASA began utilizing the SpaceX *Dragon 2* crew capsule for crewed missions. The capsule launches atop a *Falcon 9 Block 5* rocket and later returns to Earth by "splashdown," parachuting into a body of water after re-entering the atmosphere.

◆ **Virtual reality (VR)** is an alternate—albeit imaginary—world where things appear to be virtually real to the human senses of sight, hearing and touch. The illusion of these sensations is generated by a computer and based on three-dimensional environments created by a programmer.

Virtual reality is the culmination of efforts to create a fantasy reality

that is as convincing as possible. **Motion pictures** were the first step, and **3-D** (three-dimensional, or stereoscopic) motion pictures were the second step. While 3-D movies are now seen largely as a gimmick, other variations of VR, such as **flight simulators**, have had quite serious and practical applications. Developed by the Link Corporation, flight simulators were used to train pilots for the U.S. Army and Air Force in World War II. This line of development continued after the war and the computer revolution of the 1970s made it possible to create computer-generated simulations of terrain over which an airplane might fly. By 1982, the U.S. Air Force had begun work on the **Super Cockpit** or **Visually Coupled Airborne Systems Simulator (VCASS)**.

In the private sector, efforts to further develop VR have led to virtual worlds whose dimensions are limited only by the ingenuity of their creators. One inspiration for VR was the 1984 science fiction book *Neuromancer*, wherein author William Gibson describes a global computer network that provides total immersion and interactivity for participants, which he called **cyberspace**.

In 1985, a computer scientist and game creator named Jaron Lanier founded **VPL Research** in California's Silicon Valley. Lanier, who coined the term "virtual reality," wanted VPL to be the first company to create a complete virtual world. This project involved the integration of both a helmet (such as that being developed in VCASS) and a **DataGlove**, which would add a sense of touch and the capability to manipulate. VPL's first DataGlove was delivered to NASA in 1986, and the first VR environment was marketed in 1988.

By the 1990s, VR systems were being used for everything from simulated racquetball games to architectural design. In the racquetball game, one could play with a virtual ball, and in the latter, one could design a building and virtually walk around in it before it was built. If adjustments needed to be made in such a massive project, it would be much easier to do so before the actual building was constructed. By 1993, a project was underway to design a virtual map of the human body to aid doctors in surgery. In 1998, the first robotic surgery utilizing VR was performed in Paris. In 2007, Google introduced Street View, a VR service that shows frequently updated panoramic views of streets, buildings, rural areas, and other sites around the world. In the 2010s, VR for entertainment and gaming purposes became more widespread and accessible. Indeed, applications of VR in science, industry, and entertainment seem virtually endless.

The internet as we know it today grew from research and developments dating back as far as the 1960s, when the U.S. Department of Defense (DOD) began using **packet switching**, which was an early method of grouping and transmitting data over a digital network. In 1969, the DOD established the **Advanced Research Projects Agency Network (ARPANET)** as the first wide area packet-switching network, which linked computers at certain research institutions via telephone lines. In 1981, the National Science Foundation funded the **Computer Science Network (CSNET)**, expanding access to ARPANET. By the early 1990s, many more networks had been created, and because the set of rules for how to send and receive information—called the internet protocol suite—had been standardized, these networks were now able to link. On August 6, 1991, researchers at CERN, the European Organization for Nuclear Research, published the very first website on the **World Wide Web (WWW)**, and made their web browser public in January 1992. This marked the beginning of web resources becoming accessible over the internet. These resources, which could include web pages, documents, and other types of media, were—and still are—identified by **uniform resource locators (URLs)**, also known as "web addresses."

By the late 1990s, the Web was quickly becoming more widely used by people all over the world as more and more browsers and websites became available, including emailing and messaging services, forums, blogs, and online shopping websites. By 2000, the internet carried 51 percent of the information flowing through two-way telecommunication. By 2007, that figure grew to 97 percent. The rapid growth was driven in large part by the boom of community-oriented sites like YouTube, Facebook, and Wikipedia.

Following this, the rise in popularity of smartphones like the BlackBerry and Apple iPhone in the aughts made the internet mobile and further encouraged social use. The advent of video streaming services in the 2010s began to revolutionize how people accessed and consumed entertainment.

The internet is constantly growing and changing, and it will undoubtedly continue influencing human society and culture for as long as we keep using it.

Electric vehicles were first designed and created in the mid-1800s after the invention of one of the first electric motors by Hungarian physicist Ányos István Jedlik. Once rechargeable batteries that allowed for the storage of electricity on a vehicle were invented, many inventors tried creating battery-powered carriages in the late 1800s and early 1900s. However, the creation of the internal-combustion engine and mass production of gasoline- and diesel-powered automobiles rendered electric vehicle development obsolete as these new fossil fuel-based automobiles could travel farther and were cheaper to fuel and operate.

Near the end of the twentieth century, interest in a future of electric vehicles was renewed, in part due to early concerns expressed by the California Air Resources Board about the environmental impact of carbon emissions from cars. In response, many automakers developed gas/electric hybrid models or full electric models of vehicles, but consumer demand remained low and the models were not made available on the wider market.

In 2004, newly founded Tesla Motors began developing the Tesla Roadster, which was the first all-electric car to be legal to drive on the highway when it went on sale in 2008. It was able to drive more than 200 miles per charge and marked the beginning of a major push by auto manufacturers all over the world to develop and manufacture electric vehicles. And this was spurred by a growing global understanding about climate change and a desire to reduce greenhouse gas emissions among consumers. Electric cars became more widely available throughout the 2010s but remained expensive and out of reach for some. As of 2020, there were only 6.8 million electric vehicles being used in the world, though that number is expected to increase quickly in the coming decades.

The idea of altering human DNA in order to program or influence a person's traits or treat diseases has been around since the discovery and modern understanding of DNA in the mid-twentieth century. Scientists understood that genetic "mistakes," or specific sequences in DNA that cause certain traits or diseases, could be passed from parent to child, and developed technologies to minimize the chances of certain sequences being passed down. However, technology for altering the DNA of a living organism was more complicated. To correct genetic mistakes, scientists needed to be able to remove and replace certain sections of complex DNA molecules, which proved extremely difficult or impossible in some cases.

However, in 2012, American scientist Jennifer Doudna and French scientist Emmanuelle Charpentier discovered a molecular tool known as CRISPR-Cas9 (clustered regularly interspaced short palindromic repeats), which allowed scientists to "snip" out and insert DNA segments at specific locations in the sequence with unprecedented precision. The technology was soon used to modify the genomes of farm animals, plants, mice, rats, and primates. Scientists modified the genomes of bacteria-killing viruses to be more effective at destroying resistant bacteria, and scientists were even able to remove HIV from infected cells of mice.

Despite the development of this promising technology, many scientists remain concerned about the ethics and safety of altering human DNA. In 2018, a Chinese scientist announced that he had edited the genes of two human babies, having used CRISPR-Cas9 technology on them in the womb to make the twins less likely to become infected with HIV. In 2019, this technology was used to treat a patient with sickle cell anemia, a severe genetic blood disorder.

Future applications of the technology are virtually limitless. Scientists believe it could be used to cure many diseases and conditions, and it could even create new species or bring back some that have gone extinct.

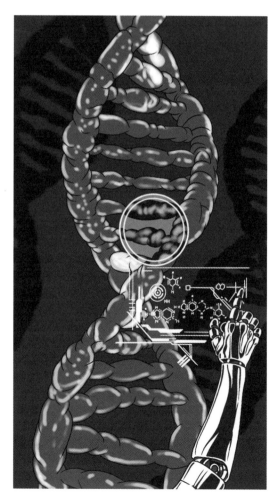

TRIVIA QUESTIONS

Test your knowledge and challenge your friends with the following questions. The answers are on the pages indicated.

1. Place the following inventions in order of their date of invention beginning with the earliest to the most recent: a) the submarine; b) Teflon; c) eyeglasses; d) electric batteries; e) fax machines. (See nos. 24, 29, 35, 70, 75)

2. Almost everyone recognizes Alexander Graham Bell as the inventor of the practical telephone. Can you name the inventor whom Bell beat to the patent office by a mere two hours? (See no. 53)

3. Name the six simple machines. (See page vii)

4. Chloroform came into widespread use as a general anesthesia after being used on this well-known person. (See no. 41)

5. The first known recording of a song was made on December 6, 1877. Name the person who performed the song and the title. (See no. 55)

6. Originally known as "artificial silk," this material was developed in response to a silkworm disease that was threatening the silk industry in France. What is this material known as today? (See no. 57)

7. On March 28, 1899, this individual sent the first international wireless message. Name the inventor and the two countries over whose borders the message traveled. (See no. 63)

8. The French Benedictine monk Gerbert d'Aurillac, who became Pope Sylvester II in 999 CE, is also known as the inventor of this device. His design used a system of gears run by counterbalanced weights. Name the invention. (See no. 20)

9. Around 1500, he drew the first functional helicopter design, but did not have the means to power his invention at the time. Name the inventor. (See no. 77)

10. Before the first water wheel-powered and wind-powered mills were built, grain was ground into flour by hand. Which source of power did millers harness first—wind or water—and how much later did they harness the other? (See no. 18)

11. This invention is one of humankind's oldest machines. It appeared in its earliest form about 3000 BCE in Mesopotamia as a sand-covered board on which marks were drawn with a finger or a stick. In fact, its name comes from an ancient word for "dust." Name the invention. (See no. 9)

12. Dating back to at least 50,000 BCE, this invention was probably the earliest complex (multiple part) weapons system. Name the invention. (See no. 5)

13. This invention was first explored by a first-century inventor known as Hero of Alexandria. He built a machine called the aeolipile. However, no one could envision a practical application for it, and the project was abandoned for over a thousand years. Finally, a Scottish engineer developed the first practical one that could not only run itself but also other machines. Name the invention and the inventor who built the first practical prototype. (See no. 32)

14. Around 260 BCE, the Greek mathematician Archimedes wrote about this invention that involves an inclined plane wrapped around a cylinder. Archimedes reputedly devised this invention as a means of irrigation. Name the invention. (See no. 15)

15. In 1869, this inventor won a $10,000 prize for inventing a replacement for ivory used in the manufacture of billiard balls. Name the inventor and the substance that he developed. (See no. 52)

16. The first commercial tape recording of a musical performance was made by BASF at their Ludwigshafen, Germany, factory on November 19, 1936. What group did this recording feature? (See no. 65)

17. In 1926, the first public television broadcast was made in this country. Name the country and the name of the inventor who built the first practical television. (See no. 69)

18. In 1679, almost three hundred years before the introduction of computers, the development of the eventual basis for all computer language had taken place. Name the system and its inventor. (See no. 78)

19. A practical commercial use was developed for this invention in 1954 when Percy LeBaron Spencer discovered that radio waves had melted a candy bar in his pocket. Name the invention. (See no. 81)

20. Name the first man-made machine to enter interstellar space in 1985. (See no. 93)

PROJECT SUGGESTIONS

1. Each invention in this book has had a dramatic impact on life as we know it. Can you imagine how different your life would be if some of these discoveries had never been made? For example, imagine how different your life would be without something as basic as the electric light. What would your house look like? What about your workplace or your downtown skyline? Would we have kerosene lamps for lighting or would something else have come along? Play the game by imagining how your life would be different and how the world would be different without any one of the one hundred inventions listed in this book.

2. Write a paper or make a display that shows how one invention made another invention possible. (Example: The waterwheel wasn't possible until the invention of the wheel.)

3. Construct models of some of the simpler inventions, such as water wheels or levers, to show how they work.

4. Construct a second model or draw a diagram to show how a task was done before the invention of a simple machine made it easier.

5. Discuss and demonstrate the importance of certain "breakthrough" inventions—such as the **steam engine**, the **internal-combustion engine,** or the **transistor**—and how these paved the way for many other inventions that would not have been possible without them.

INDEX

OUT NOW: